H. P. Wood

Illustrated by David Clark

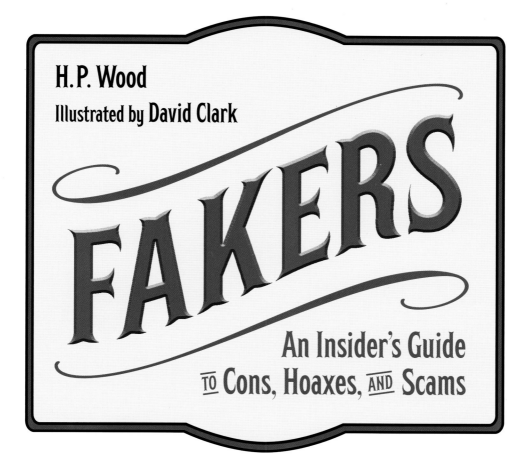

FAKERS

An Insider's Guide to Cons, Hoaxes, and Scams

Charlesbridge

*For Mark, my unindicted co-conspirator*
*—H.P. Wood*

Published by Charlesbridge
85 Main Street
Watertown, MA 02472
(617) 926-0329
www.charlesbridge.com

**Library of Congress Cataloging-in-Publication Data**
Names: Wood, H.P. (Hilary Poole), author.
Title: Fakers: an insider's guide to cons, hoaxes, and scams / H.P. Wood; illustrated
    by David Clark.
Description: Watertown, MA : Charlesbridge, [2018]
Identifiers: LCCN 2017033089 (print) | LCCN 2017035371 (ebook) | ISBN
    9781632895653 (ebook) | ISBN 9781632895660 (ebook pdf) | ISBN
    9781580897433 (reinforced for library use)
Subjects: LCSH: Hoaxes—Juvenile literature. | Swindlers and swindling—Juvenile
    literature. | Fraud—Juvenile literature.
Classification: LCC HV6691 (ebook) | LCC HV6691 .P59 2018 (print) | DDC
    364.16/3—dc23
LC record available at https://lccn.loc.gov/2017033089

Printed in China
(hc) 10 9 8 7 6 5 4 3 2 1

Illustrations done in traditional and digital media
Display type set in Herschel Creamline by Brian Brubaker
Text type set in Garamond Pro by Adobe Systems Incorporated
Color separations by Colourscan Print Co Pte Ltd, Singapore
Printed by 1010 Printing International Limited in Huizhou, Guangdong, China
Production supervision by Brian G. Walker
Designed by Diane M. Earley

# CONTENTS

# INTRODUCTION

## A Tale as Old as Time

There's no way to know when the first scam took place. I like to imagine that one of our prehistoric ancestors convinced another to trade his collection of shells for a "really great cave" just over the next hill.[1]

Whatever occurred, we know this much for sure: humans have been tricking one another for a very long time. That's no surprise. But what is amazing is that many of the earliest scams are still in use today. And the basic premise behind every scam—deceiving someone to get something you want from them—is much older still.

### The Wild Kingdom

Humans have invented tons of tremendous things. There's the wheel, of course. And antibiotics. The internal combustion engine. Stuffed-crust pizza. Instagram.

---

[1] Spoiler alert: there was no cave over the next hill.

But one thing humans did *not* invent is deception. The animal kingdom is home to quite a large number of accomplished fakers. Different animals carry out their deceptions in different ways. One of the most basic forms of deception is camouflage. Camouflage is why grasshoppers are green, while leopards have spots. When a branch of the bear family slowly migrated north, their hair got lighter, the better to blend in with their new, snowy environment.[2] Another example is how stripes help zebras avoid being eaten by lions. You might think that their black-and-white coloring would make zebras stand out against the long grasses of their habitat. But lions are colorblind! When a lion looks at a herd of zebras, all it can see is a mass of waving lines.

Basic coloration is just the beginning of animal deception. Some animals can actually change color—the chameleon is famous for it, of course, but cuttlefish, squid, and octopuses can do it as well. Certain types of spiders and beetles can, too.

Other animals go even further, using trickery to fool their prey. For example, a Central American snake called the cantil (similar to a cottonmouth) has a little white bit on its tail that looks like a worm. Birds and frogs try to catch the worm, only to realize too late that they are the cantil's dinner instead. Similarly, the deep-sea anglerfish has a lure on the top of its head that it uses to attract smaller fish. When a little fish touches the lure, the angler's jaw snaps shut automatically. The green heron is even smarter: it deliberately drops small bits of bait into the water to attract fish, and when the fish come to the surface to eat, they become food.

Some animals are even good actors. You've probably heard how the opossum is famous for playing dead to escape predators. A number of birds, including grouse, killdeer, some plovers, and the mourning dove,

---

[2] By the way, polar bear hair is not really white—it's transparent. It just looks white, both to human eyes and to seal eyes. (Unfortunately for seals.)

will put on what scientists call a distraction display—limping around
and squawking as though they are
injured—in order to lure predators
away from their nests. In Mexico a
small jungle cat called a margay
mimics the cries of baby monkeys.
When the adult monkeys come to
check on their young, the margay
attacks and eats them.

But the cleverest animals of all
may be the ones that can trick other
animals into doing their bidding. The
cuckoo bird, for example, lays its eggs in other birds' nests and lets the
other birds do all the work of feeding and carrying for their young. Some
types of ants do the cuckoo one better: slave-maker ants enter the colonies
of other ants, changing their scents to mask their approach. Once inside,
they take the other colony's larvae prisoner and bring the babies back to
their own colony to serve as slaves.[3]

## What's Your Point?

I know what you're thinking: Why am I reading about animal fakers? I
thought this book was about con artists! Don't worry; you haven't been
scammed. But it's worth noticing how similar the many techniques of
con artists are to the many ways animals deceive each other.

Want to see some human camouflage? Check out chapter 5, which is
packed full of impostors. A woman named Cassie Chadwick blended
right in with the upper crust of the early nineteenth century, convincing

---

[3] Occasionally the slave ants rebel and kill their overseers. I am not even kidding; this is really a thing.

everyone she was an heiress when she was nothing of the sort. About eighty years later a young hustler by the name of David Hampton scammed New York City's rich and famous simply by pretending he was one of them. And then there was iconic financial scammer Charles Ponzi, who specialized in appearing so fabulously wealthy that you'd never imagine he was robbing you.

Or how about the lure technique—those animals that offer something tempting to draw in their unsuspecting prey? Frankly, anyone who's ever played three-card monte, listened carefully to a pyramid scheme, or responded to a Nigerian prince's email is no smarter than the little fish that cozy up to an angler right until its jaws go snap.

And those truly deceitful animals we discussed—like the cuckoos and the slave-maker ants? They have a lot in common with the handiwork of Thierry Tilly. He managed to convince a family of French aristocrats that they were targeted for murder, and that their only salvation was to turn over all their money, abandon their château, and take jobs at Burger King in order to support Tilly. Slave-maker ant, indeed!

## Only Human

For all our similarities to animal deceivers, though, there are certain abilities humans have that most other species don't. A big one is the ability to entertain one another. Sure, our cousins in the primate family know how to have a good time, and some researchers are convinced that dogs can understand certain types of humor. But has a chimpanzee ever carved a ten-foot giant out of stone just to win an argument? Do dogs sit around trying to impress one another by guessing each other's birthdays?[4] Doubt it.

---

[4] Check out chapter 3 for the story of the Cardiff Giant and some tips on how those carnies at county fairs are able to guess your weight, age, or birth month.

Animals have an impressive range of skills for deception, but only humans understand what the great P. T. Barnum called "humbug." Humbug refers to the idea of deception as entertainment. Whether it's magic, spoon bending, tarot-card reading, or creating fake aliens for fun and profit, humans are uniquely wired for all manner of deception. And we use our scamming abilities for a whole range of reasons—not just for entertainment, but also to gain advantage in war, and to gain financial advantage as well. We have even put our faith in quack doctors because we desperately want their empty promises to come true.

In this book you will encounter all these types of fakers and many more. You will learn how they do it, and you'll be asked to contemplate why people are so eager to be fooled. I promise you'll become an expert on cons, hoaxes, and scams in no time.

But, please, I beg of you: use your hoaxing powers for good, not evil. And afterward, be sure to write and tell me all about it for a sequel.

# CHAPTER 1

## Conjurers and Con Artists: Short Cons

The most durable cons are usually the simplest: the short cons. Short cons are scams that happen very quickly and usually involve small amounts of money. A short con can be a man making cards dance across a cardboard box. A short con can be a "fantastic deal" on a stolen TV. A short con can take the form of a stranger who simply bumps into you, accidentally on purpose, and suddenly your wallet's gone. Twenty-first-century scammers dress up their cons in modern trappings, but at the end of the day, they are following in the footsteps of many generations of rogues that came before them.

### The Shell Game

The shell game used to be called cups and balls, and its origins go all the way back to ancient Rome. Actually, some have claimed the game is even older than that. There is an illustration on the wall of an ancient Egyptian tomb that appears to show people engaged in an activity that looks a whole lot like cups and balls.

In this age-old trick, the performer has several cups and several balls, and he seems to make the balls appear and disappear under various cups and in various combinations. Performers use methods like sleight of hand, which is when the performer moves an object so quickly that the audience doesn't notice, and misdirection, which is when the performer intentionally distracts the audience. All the jibber-jabbering that magicians do, for example—which they call "patter"—is a form of misdirection. The idea is to get viewers to pay attention to anything other than what's actually going on with the trick itself.

Cups and balls became popular in Europe during the Middle Ages. A painting called *The Conjurer* by Hieronymus Bosch[5] shows a magician (or conjurer) performing some version of the cups-and-balls act (*see painting right*). But if you look closely at Bosch's painting, you'll see something very interesting. The real action is not happening on the right, where the conjurer is; it's happening on the left, in the audience. Look at the fellow with glasses, who is staring up at the sky, innocent as can be: his hand is reaching for the other fellow's money pouch. Then look at the man in black with his arm around the lady in red: his hand is going for her necklace. There are *at least* four pickpockets in the image.[6]

By the nineteenth century, cups and balls had come to be known as thimblerig. The cups were now thimbles (little caps that people wear on their fingers while sewing), and the balls had become a single pea. But the really important development was that thimblerig was played for money.

The performer—no longer a *con*jurer but a *con* artist—placed the pea under one of three thimbles. Then he would smoothly slide the thimbles

---

[5] Bosch was a Dutch painter who lived from around 1450 to 1516. Interesting guy—he once did a painting of a man playing a flute with his butt.

[6] Two pickpockets are working on the man who's studying the magician; the man in black is reaching for the woman in red's necklace; and the man in green is sliding his hand up the sleeve of the man in brown. That fellow at the way back of the crowd looks a little shifty as well, but I can't prove anything.

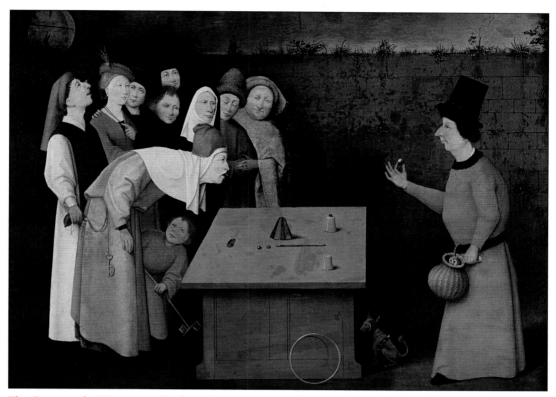

The Conjurer *by Hieronymus Bosch (c. 1502) shows a performer keeping an audience distracted while they are robbed.*

around to rearrange their order. After the thimbles had been moved a few times, onlookers (or suckers, in our terms) would be invited to place bets on which thimble was hiding the pea.

Which thimble hid the pea? None of them. The con artist had already "palmed" the pea, hiding it in his hand. That way, when an audience member chose a thimble, the con artist could slip the pea into it—or not. This ensured that he was always in control of whether the bettors won or—far more often—lost.

The trick became known as the shell game when American con artists switched to walnut shells rather than thimbles. Frequently the con artist would hold a wad of cash in one hand while he did the trick. The money served two purposes: one, it hid the pea from view, and two, it served as a distraction for the audience.

In the twenty-first century, the shell game is more often played with bottle caps. These days, performers don't necessarily palm the pea. They are able to control where the pea ends up by sliding it out from under one shell and back under another so quickly that you can't see it happen. But the trick is the same. And here's the key point: you will not win.

JEFFERSON "SOAPY" SMITH

One of the greatest thimblerig operators was a con man named Jefferson "Soapy" Smith. The nickname Soapy came from Smith's prize-package racket, which involved selling soap on street corners. Smith would pull a bar of soap from his bag and reveal to potential customers that the soap was wrapped in a twenty-, fifty-, or one-hundred-dollar bill. Smith had a whole case of soap wrapped just the same way. People would spend five dollars apiece on soap that actually cost about fifty cents, all in the hope that theirs might also have a hundred-dollar bill wrapped around it.[7]

But Smith is remembered most for his skill as a thimblerigger. The story goes that he lost at thimblerig only once. A man calmly placed a gun on the table and said, "Soapy, I'm not going to tell you which shell has the pea; I'm going to tell you which shells *don't* have the pea." Seeing as how Smith had palmed the pea—meaning *none* of the shells had it—this was a great strategy. Soapy knew when he'd been beaten. He took one look at the gun and let the man have his money.

Soapy was only thirty-eight years old when he died. He was shot down in a confrontation with a group of angry gold miners in Skagwell, Alaska. Looking back on it, maybe he should have let people win more often.

[7] It would not.

## Find the Lady

A game that's closely related to the shell game is called three-card monte. But as more than one practitioner has pointed out, three-card monte is less of a game and more of a mugging.

A card scam similar to three-card monte was first recorded in 1408. But three-card monte as we know it found its most fertile ground in the second half of the 1800s, on riverboats, at racetracks, and in the saloons of the Wild West.

Here's how it works. There are three cards: two numbered cards and the queen of hearts (sometimes referred to as "the lady"). The dealer puts the cards faceup, points out where the queen is, and then turns the cards over and moves them around. Like the shell game, where the goal is to find the pea, the goal in three-card monte is to find the queen. And like the shell game, the only time you'll find her is when the dealer lets you find her on purpose.

Three-card monte depends on a sleight-of-hand trick that is simple to understand but not easy to do well. When the dealer picks up the cards to move them around, he picks up a single card in one hand and two cards in the other hand—one on top of the other. This seems like a totally natural thing for him to do. He's only got the two hands, after all! But the secret of three-card monte lies in the hand that's got two cards.

Let's say we have Card A, Card B, and Card Q (for the queen). The operator shows them to us, then lays them out in a row, in the following order: Card A, Card Q, Card B. Then he flips the cards over, so they are facedown. We feel pretty good, because we know that the queen is in the middle. With his left hand, the dealer picks up Card A. With his right hand, he picks up Card B first and then Card Q. *OK*, we think, *the queen is in his right hand, underneath Card B.*

Then he throws the cards down on the box in a different order, to rearrange them. You will naturally assume that he drops Card Q first, because it's on the bottom and that would be the logical way to do it. But that's when he's got you. A skilled dealer can control which of the two cards he throws down first. So, even if you are watching *very* closely, you simply can't know whether he threw down Card Q and then Card B, or Card B and then Card Q. The sleight of hand is so subtle that you would need a slow-motion camera to spot which card falls where.

*OK, that's cool*, you're thinking, *but if I know that it's either of those two cards in his right hand, then I have a fifty-fifty chance of choosing correctly. Right?*

Well, maybe? Except . . . no. No, you don't. And here's why.

If the game were simply a matter of choosing between two or even three cards, it would stand to reason that you would occasionally beat the dealer, just due to the law of averages. But three-card monte dealers are not in the business of being beaten. So there are multiple layers of deceptions happening all at the same time.

First, most of the people watching the game—maybe *all* of the people—are not innocent audience members. They actually work for the dealer; they're called *shills*. A shill's one and only job is to get you—the sucker—to put your money on the table. Shills will happily play all kinds of mind tricks, just to make you think the game is skewed in your favor.

For example, one trick involves one shill momentarily distracting the dealer, so that another shill can bend the corner of the queen card. But it's not just that: the shill then *shows you* that the card is bent. That gets you thinking that you've got a sure bet: you'll always know where the queen is, because you saw the shill mark the card. The dealer might think he is cheating you, but you are actually cheating him. Genius!

Except, remember: the card bender works for the dealer; they planned this trick in advance. While tossing the cards, the dealer subtly *un*bends the queen and bends another card instead . . . causing you to bet on the wrong card. You lose again. And what are you gonna do, complain? Not likely. To complain would mean admitting not only that you are a cheater, but also that you are a lousy cheater.

But let's say you avoid the mind games of any shills. Let's say you are very clever or just extremely lucky, and you put your money down on the correct card. You bet on the queen. The operator just hands you your winnings and says, "Congratulations," right?

Nope. The moment you do that, one of the shills is going to put a higher bet on the *wrong* card. The dealer will accept the higher bet and reject your bet. "Only one player at a time, please," he'll say.

If that doesn't work, someone (another shill, naturally) will say, "The cops are coming, the cops are coming!" and the entire game will evaporate quicker than you can say . . . well . . . the cops are coming.

> *"Three-card monte is not a game of chance. Three-card monte is not a game of skill. Three-card monte is not a game."*
> —*Ricky Jay,*
> **Celebrations of Curious Characters**

Some suckers have ended up having to convince police officers that *they* weren't the ones running the monte game in the first place!

And if nothing else, don't forget the Hieronymus Bosch painting from earlier. While you are trying to be clever by beating the dealer, somebody else may be cleverly helping himself to the contents of your pockets.

## Pig in a Poke

Say what you will about shell-game operators and three-card monte-dealers, but at least there is a skill involved.[8] Those gentlemen—they *are* typically men—are crooks. But they are crooks with a skill.

Lots of classic short cons, however, require no skills of any kind. Consider the Pig in a Poke scam, which is at least four hundred years old. Back in the day, food was harder to get than it is now. There was no Ye Olde Wal-Marte where you could go pick up a few things on the way home from the joust. And meat was especially prized. The Pig in a Poke scam involved the scammer selling a tasty pig all wrapped up in a bag (or a poke) and ready to take home. When it was time to start cooking, the buyer (or sucker) would open the bag to find a dead cat instead.[9] Cats have many attributes, but tastiness is not one of them.

These days it's pretty rare to find someone who'll buy a dead pig from a stranger, even at a steep discount. But a gaming console? A T V? A cell phone? Now you're talking.

The modern twist on a Pig in a Poke scam involves selling a desirable product—let's say the latest model of Nintendo gaming console. The scammer says, "Hey, buddy, I happen to have a car full of brand-new Nintendos

---

[8] Go get a pack of cards and try to deal two cards out of the same hand without giving away whether you are throwing the top card or the bottom. Hang on . . . finish the chapter first! But then you should definitely try this: it's not as easy as it might sound.

[9] This scam is where the expression "letting the cat out of the bag" comes from.

that I need to get rid of. I'll sell you one cheap . . . How about fifty bucks?"

The product sells for several times that, so fifty bucks sounds pretty good to you. Off you go to claim your prize from the scammer's car. And there they are, stacks of Nintendos, still in their boxes. You study one of them. The packaging is perfect; the weight feels right. What a deal! You feel very proud of yourself for making such a good bargain.

You will feel considerably less proud when you get home, open the box, and discover that you've just bought fifty bucks' worth of old newspapers and just enough rocks to make the weight seem right.

Sorry, friend, you just bought a Nintendo in a poke.

## Melon Drop

I know what you're thinking. *What dummy falls for that Pig in a Poke scam?* Because if those Nintendos *aren't* fake, they are definitely stolen, so only a fool would buy one in the first place.

You may have a point. But optimism is a powerful thing. So is greed. People want to believe that luck has favored them. They want to believe they got a good deal. You'd be surprised how many people have fallen for scams exactly like this over the past few hundred years. There's a reason scammers keep doing it: *it keeps working!*

Even if you are too smart to fall for the Pig in a Poke scam, don't be so sure that you can't be "gotten" some other way. Sometimes you don't have to be optimistic or greedy. Sometimes you just have to be in the right place at the wrong time.

Consider the classic Melon Drop scam. You're walking along in a crowd, minding your own business. Suddenly—seemingly out of nowhere—you collide with a stranger. The collision causes the stranger to drop a package that he or she is carrying, which turns out to be something extremely valuable. The package is now broken and it's your fault. The person protests, loudly, and insists you make good on whatever it was you carelessly destroyed.

Except the whole thing is a con. You didn't "carelessly" do anything. The scammer very carefully chose you and made sure that you two walked

## THE DICE CON

Bunco is a dice game that was invented in England several hundred years ago. Originally it was a very polite game that respectable young ladies could play. But it was brought to America by some unnamed swindler, and before long, the word *bunco* lost all semblance of respectability. There were "bunco parlors" where you could gamble and usually lose, and "bunco gangs" made up of groups of con artists working in tandem. (Soapy Smith [see page 4] had his own bunco gang, for example.) The word *bunco* is now used to describe any kind of swindle or con.

But the World Bunco Association would like you to know that there remains, to this day, a highly respectable dice game of bunco. According to their website, it is "a great way to maintain relationships and make new friends."

I'm sure Soapy Smith would agree!

into each other. And whatever you supposedly broke either is not valuable or was broken already.

Accusing someone of breaking something that was already broken is a very old short con. These days, a fairly common method involves a minor car accident, in which the car that supposedly got damaged was already a mess long before the accident.

Since this is kind of an obvious scam, you might be wondering why the Melon Drop has such a specific name. Glad you asked!

Fruit tends to be very expensive in Japan, in great part because of the way it is grown there. Perfect fruit is a luxury item. There was a time when even regular old melons cost upward of a hundred dollars.

Understanding this, con artists in Europe and the United States would buy a melon for a few bucks (or pounds, or euros) at the local grocer and then go hunting for some unsuspecting Japanese tourists. Crash go the people, smash goes the melon, and suddenly the tourists are being hit up for fifty or one hundred dollars to replace the *very valuable* produce that was destroyed.

Whether it's a melon drop, a rigged dice game, or a fast-paced round of three-card monte, the secret of every short con is keeping the interaction brief. Short cons happen so quickly that by the time the victim realizes he's been taken, the scammer is already gone.

The downside for the con artist is that big scores are hard to come by. After all, if you are going to interact with your marks for only five to ten minutes, how much money can you possibly get them to hand over? More ambitious con artists need to spend more time with their victims, spinning elaborate stories to cover their scams. That brings us to the more complex undertakings of the long con.

# CHAPTER 2

## Just Trust Me: Long Cons

The opposite of the short con, which usually takes place in the blink of an eye, is the long con. Long cons are complicated scams that take time. They often involve false identities, phony paperwork, and elaborate backstories. While short cons involve tricking someone for a minute or two, long cons can take months or even years to play out. Getting away with a long con is *much* trickier. Indeed, plenty of people don't—as you're about to discover.

### The Spanish Prisoner

*Kind Sir:*

*We have never met, but your reputation for generosity is well known. With that in mind, I write to you on a matter of great urgency.*

*It is my sad duty to report that the Honorable Marquess of Milford Haven, a fine young man and the great-grandson of Princess Alice, Grand Duchess of Hesse, has been kidnapped by the treacherous Spanish. I ask your discretion in keeping this matter secret. The Marquess's very life depends upon it.*

*I am hoping you will be so kind and noble as to make a modest contribution to a private fund that will finance a rescue mission. The young man's family will be most grateful for your assistance and will surely make you a very rich man . . .*

Dating back to the mid-1800s, the Spanish Prisoner is the granddaddy of all long cons. The scam involves convincing the mark (that is, the victim) that a prominent person has been kidnapped. The scammer asks for a small sum of money—sometimes to pay as ransom, other times to help fund a rescue attempt. It is suggested that the kidnapped person or his

## LOST IN SPACE

There are a few reasons so many people enjoy hearing (or, ahem, reading!) about con artists. One is that con artists tend to be extremely creative. It's pretty amazing to see what they come up with. Taken as a form of short fiction, Nigerian emails can be absolutely delightful. There are entire websites where you can enjoy reading all the wild claims these fraudsters have made.

For my money—none of which I have given to email scammers—the best of all has to be a letter that circulated in 2016, from one Dr. Bakare Tunde. In the letter Tunde claims to be a relative of Major Abacha Tunde, who supposedly was the first African in space. The email claims that back in 1989, Tunde was sent to a top-secret Soviet space station called Salyut 8T. But he was abandoned there when the Soviet Union collapsed, and poor Tunde has been lost in space ever since! A fund-raising effort is currently under way to rescue him. Luckily the Nigerian astronaut[10] has been collecting paychecks the entire time; he has nearly thirty years' worth tucked away at the Lagos National Savings and Trust. So there is quite a bit of reward money available to the kind individual who'll help bring Tunde back to Earth. *Will it be you?*

---

[10] Nigeria does have a space program, which hopes to launch humans into space by 2030. And believe it or not, there is a kernel of truth to this scam: a cosmonaut named Sergei Krikalev was, indeed, stuck on the space station Mir due to the collapse of the Soviet Union, but only for four months.

family will be so grateful that the mark's investment will be repaid many times over.

But wait! Oh no! The rescue attempt went wrong! Or the ransom was increased, or some other disaster occurred. More money is required. There is another rescue attempt, or another ransom paid, followed by another crisis that requires more money. The con artist continues to invent new problems, which are followed by new excuses. The cycle continues until the mark either wises up or runs out of money.

The Spanish Prisoner has evolved over the years. The details of the situation often change—it doesn't have to be Spain necessarily. It doesn't even need to involve a kidnapping. Scammers will creatively use whatever situation seems believable at the time. A more recent version involves a wealthy man from a war-torn country—claiming to be a general, a prince, or some such—who needs help retrieving his vast fortune. Or there might be a helpless (and of course very pretty) young woman involved. Instead of asking for direct payments, modern Spanish Prisoner scams often ask that you surrender your bank-account information—the better to receive the many millions of reward dollars that are (never) coming your way.

Scammers based in Nigeria are famous for their outrageous emails. But their bad grammar and wild claims are not accidental. They write that way on purpose. Why? Because they only want the most gullible people to respond. If you are hip enough to recognize an email scam, Nigerian scammers don't want to talk to you anyway. But despite the name, not all Nigerian emails actually come from Nigeria. Almost as many originate from the United States!

The basic concept of the scam hasn't changed in 150 years: a wealthy person has some problem that can be solved only through access to your bank-account number. The question is, why does it continue to work? Like most long cons, the Spanish Prisoner preys on several human weaknesses. The first and most important is greed. The mark offers his money in hopes of a much greater payday in the future. Another weakness is pride, because the mark does not want to admit that he might have made a mistake, and so he keeps paying.

Sadly the Spanish Prisoner relies on a third weakness, which is compassion. The desire to help others is not usually a bad thing. But devious people can exploit that desire, taking advantage of their mark's good nature. The idea of helping others while getting rich at the same time can be irresistible. That's why the Spanish Prisoner will not go away anytime soon.

## How Much Is That Doggy in the Window?

The Internet is an amazing technology, or, really, a collection of technologies, that has completely transformed our world and improved people's lives in countless ways.

But . . .

The truth is, the Internet hasn't just improved *your* life; it has also improved the lives of con artists. Nowadays people take part in all kinds of activities online—from shopping to looking for work to falling in love—without meeting the person on the other side of the transaction. For long-con artists, this has opened up opportunities that are, literally, too vast to cover in this one book.

The basic concept of the Spanish Prisoner and Nigerian email con is this: give me a little money now, and I will give you something you want later. The "something you want" doesn't necessarily have to be money. It could be a job or an apartment. It could even be a pet.

The American Kennel Club has issued strong warnings about how dog lovers need to be careful buying puppies online. The story of a typical puppy con will sound embarrassingly familiar to you by this point. There's an initial contact about the pet, including cute pictures to get the mark to really fall in love with it. The mark pays for the dog, but just before delivery, *whoops*, more money is needed. Maybe the dog needs medical treatment. Maybe there is a problem with delivery that requires more money. The scammer will keep this cycle going as long as possible. But alas, there is no actual puppy waiting at the end.[11]

A similar scam uses the idea of lottery winnings. People receive letters announcing that—surprise!—they've won a lottery they never knew they'd entered. A large sum of money will be coming to them, but first they need to pay some sort of fee. Of course once the fee is paid, the lottery winnings never arrive. Sometimes the check does arrive, but when the person tries to cash it, she discovers it's fake. The official name for this type of scam is advance-fee fraud.

*Sure, he's adorable, but make sure he really exists before you hand over your money.*

To borrow an old phrase, there are as many types of advance-fee fraud as there are stars in the sky. Fake recruiters have charged unemployed people a fee to find them jobs that never materialize. Scammers have posed as lonely single women who then "borrow" money from lovestruck men. Con artists have stolen from students while "helping" them apply for college scholarships that don't exist. (You can read more about fake scholarships in the conclusion of this book. *Discipulum emptor!* Student beware!)

If you are ever involved in a financial transaction with a stranger and that person suddenly needs "just a little money up front," it's a good idea to be suspicious. Of course everything may be fine. But make sure you

---

[11] Nor is there a kitten, parrot, iguana, or whatever "hook" the scammer used.

do your homework on whatever institution or company the stranger claims to represent. And remember: just because a website looks real, that doesn't make it so.

## Building a Pyramid

The long cons we've looked at so far involve a fraudster targeting one specific person. But there are far more ambitious long cons out there. One of the most common involves a type of investment called a pyramid scheme.

Pyramid schemes are not as old as the actual pyramids, but they have been around for a very long time. Con artists are always coming up with new backstories to try to make *their* schemes appear unique. But at the end of the day, they are all putting lipstick on the same pig.

Here's how a pyramid scheme works: Let's say I come to you and say, "Hey, buddy, I'm starting this great new business called H. P. Wood's Pet Rocks. I have these awesome rocks that are going to be incredibly popular and make tons of money. I just need a little cash to start the business. Since we're friends, I'm going to let you in on the ground floor."

So you say sure, and you give me a hundred dollars to be the first investor. Next your job is to go get five friends to invest as well. Each of your friends gives you a hundred bucks—or five hundred total. You give me half of their investments to support our pet rock business ($250), and you get to keep the other half as a commission. This seems great because you've made net profit of $150![12]

---

[12] It's important to understand the difference between gross and net profits. The gross profit is the total amount a person or business takes in, while the net is the gross minus all expenses (aka, what the person or business actually gets to keep). In this case, your gross is the $500 your friends gave you, while your net is $500 minus the $100 you paid me to join the scheme *and* the $250 you gave me in profit sharing. That means you netted $150 for your efforts while I netted $350 for almost no effort at all . . . which is why you're going to be mad at me when this is over.

Then your five friends each go out and find more friends to invest. Let's assume each of your five friends recruits five people—that's twenty-five new investors. Each one pays a hundred dollars ($2,500 total). The recruiters get to keep a small commission and then they pass the money along to you; you also get a commission, and then you pass the rest to me. The twenty-five new investors find *more* people to invest—and again, they keep a little money and pass the rest along. The money flows from the bottom of the pyramid (that is, the new investors) to the top (me!).

Pyramid schemes always collapse eventually, for two reasons. First, sooner or later, we will run out of people willing to give us a hundred dollars. Second, eventually somebody is going to say, "Hey, wait a minute. Weren't we supposed to be selling pet rocks? What happened to all the profits from the pet rocks?" Of course, there never were any pet rocks.

It is around this time that H. P. Wood abruptly leaves town.

I've made pyramid schemes sound pretty simple here . . . so simple that you might be wondering why anyone falls for a con that's built on such an obviously shaky foundation. But it's important to understand that pyramid schemes don't arrive in a box marked LONG CON INSIDE. Instead they are presented as "work-at-home" plans, nutritional supplement franchises, or secretive "insider" stock market tips. Any job or investment that requires members to do a lot of recruiting should be viewed skeptically, to say the least.

Alas, when it comes to getting rich, skeptics are in short supply. In fact, pyramid schemes are not just an issue in the United States; they are a global problem, too. In one dramatic example, a series of interconnected pyramid schemes destroyed the entire economy of Albania when the schemes all collapsed simultaneously in 1997. A major reason things got so out of control was that there was essentially no private property in Albania until 1991. When the Soviet Union collapsed that year, Albanians found themselves in a brave new world of market economies—buying and selling and trading in totally unfamiliar ways. In other words, regular Albanians had basically zero understanding of how investing works, which made them perfect targets for scammers. The schemes ensnared more than two hundred thousand citizens who lost the equivalent of $1.2 billion, and the resulting crisis led to a violent overthrow of the Albanian government.

## Mr. Ponzi

The most famous long con of our time began in a very simple way. It all started with office furniture.

Carlo Ponzi was born in 1882 in Lugo, Italy. He emigrated to the United States at age twenty-one, arriving in New York City with—as he later told a reporter—"$2.50 in cash and $1 million in hopes." But Ponzi, who now went by Charles, spent the next decade getting into scrapes with the law in both America and Canada. He served jail time in both countries due to various small-time crimes, including writing bad checks. At one point he served time in the same Atlanta jail as Charles Morse, a super-wealthy Wall Street investor who'd been imprisoned for "misappropriating funds" (aka ripping off his investors). Morse's example made Ponzi realize he'd been thinking too small.

After his release, Ponzi ended up in Boston, where he rented an office space and filled it with expensive furniture. Ponzi wanted to look wealthier than he was, because he believed that money flows most easily to those who *appear* to already have it. Unfortunately he had no way of actually paying for all those chairs and desks. This put him into conflict with a furniture dealer named Joseph Daniels. Daniels went to Ponzi's office in a rage, demanding the return of either the money (which Ponzi didn't have) or the furniture (which Ponzi didn't want to part with). But Ponzi managed to turn a problem into an opportunity—he had a new idea for a company, and Daniels would soon become his first investor.

The scheme involved something called International Reply Coupons (IRCs). Nowadays we take the idea of international mail for granted, but in the early 1900s it was still sort of a new idea. How could people in, say, America and Italy exchange mail when there was no way for Americans to buy Italian stamps or vice versa? At that time, the answer was IRCs, which could be redeemed for stamps in any nation. Ponzi realized that because currency exchange rates are variable, it was possible to buy IRCs in one country, exchange them for stamps in another, and pocket the difference in value. With enough IRCs, a person could start earning a substantial return on his investment. To start the scheme rolling, Ponzi talked Daniels into loaning him one hundred dollars—mind you, this is a "loan" of a hundred dollars that Ponzi *already* owed him!

In early 1920 Ponzi opened the Securities Exchange Company. He claimed that by exploiting the exchange rates of various countries, he could pay investors 50 percent interest in forty-five days, and a full 100 percent in ninety days. Amazingly, it seemed to work! The writer Neal O'Hara declared that if five-dollar bills were snowflakes, "Ponzi

> *"The scene deployed before me [outside my office], as I alighted from my car, is something that no man could forget. To the crowd there assembled, I was the realization of their dreams. The idol. The hero. The master and arbiter of their lives. Of their hopes. Of their fortunes. The discoverer of wealth and happiness. The 'wizard' who could turn a pauper into a millionaire overnight!"*
> —Charles Ponzi, The Rise of Mr. Ponzi: **The Autobiography of a Financial Genius**

would be a three-day blizzard." The morning after Ponzi was profiled in the *Boston Post*, the streets outside his office were quite literally lined with people trying to hand him their money. Many people gave him their life savings, often many thousands of dollars. One newspaper boy invested just ten dollars, which was everything he had. Ponzi took it all.

But Ponzi wasn't buying very many IRCs. The complexities involved in purchasing the coupons, sending them to various countries, buying stamps, and then somehow exchanging those stamps for cash were totally impractical. So he didn't bother actually doing what he claimed the business was established to do. Like a pyramid scheme, the Security Exchange Company's only income was derived from new people investing in it. But in a pyramid scheme, income is distributed along the investment chain. Ponzi's scheme was different: the only investor Ponzi regularly paid was himself.

Occasionally an investor would go to Ponzi and demand to be paid the earnings (or "return") on his investment. When that happened, Ponzi would pay that investor by dipping into the money he was taking from other investors. But there were never any *actual* profits, because there was never a real stamp-exchange business in the first place.

Ponzi was never able to work out his problems with Joseph Daniels the furniture guy, and Daniels sued Ponzi for one million dollars. But instead of causing concern among investors, the lawsuit made people believe that Ponzi must be a great businessman. After all, only really successful people get sued for such large amounts of money.

But the wild success of Ponzi's scheme eventually brought about his downfall. Ponzi's company was collecting more than two hundred thousand dollars in investments per day, all of it with the promise of 100 percent return in ninety days. *Boston Post* reporters began to wonder how that much cash could be generated by simply buying and selling stamps. They asked financial expert Clarence Barron to analyze Ponzi's claims. Barron estimated that more than 150 million IRCs would need to be bought for Ponzi's plan to work. Ponzi hadn't bought anywhere near that many.

When news leaked out, there was a "run" on Ponzi's Securities Exchange Company—that's an expression for when a lot of investors all show up at the same time demanding their money. Ponzi was able to hold them off for a while, handing out coffee and doughnuts on the street outside his office. He paid back two million dollars in cash within just three days, in an attempt to reassure his investors that everything was fine.

## BERNIE MADOFF

Charles Ponzi's Ponzi scheme was a big deal at the time, but modern scammers have taken in many more people for much larger sums. The "wealth manager" Bernie Madoff stole about $65 *billion* from his clients over several decades. Some of the victims included celebrities like the actor John Malkovich and baseball great Sandy Koufax, plus—most appallingly—many charities that had invested income with Madoff's firm. Madoff is currently serving 150 years in prison for securities fraud, mail fraud, perjury, and other charges.

In a 2010 article in *New York* magazine, Madoff is described as bragging about how he convinced an elderly woman to invest what little money she had in his Ponzi scheme. A fellow prisoner offered his opinion that, speaking as a criminal himself, stealing from little old ladies was a "messed up"[13] thing to do.

"Well," Madoff said with a shrug, "that's what I did."

---

[13] The prisoner's language may have been slightly more colorful.

*Ponzi waves goodbye to America as authorities send him back to Italy.*

Everything was not fine. Ponzi's criminal past was exposed in the pages of the *Boston Post*; the paper eventually won a Pulitzer Prize for their takedown. Regulators stepped in, and Ponzi was charged with eighty-six counts of mail fraud. He was sent to prison until 1934, at which point he was immediately deported back to Italy. Meanwhile no fewer than six banks failed due to more than twenty million dollars in Ponzi-related losses (that's more than $220 million in twenty-first-century dollars). And the people who had invested their hard-earned money with Ponzi? They ended up receiving only thirty cents for every dollar they had given him.

Interestingly, if Ponzi had actually done what he claimed—that is, bought IRCs in one country and then exchanged them in a different country with a better exchange rate—his scheme would have been perfectly legal. It's a pretty basic method of making profit: you buy goods at one price and then resell them at a higher one. It happens all the time in business. What made Ponzi's scheme a "Ponzi scheme" wasn't the buying and selling of stamps; it was the fact that the buying and selling didn't actually occur.

## The Globe Tower

It was to be the largest steel structure in the world—at seven hundred feet tall, it would be three times larger than any existing building in New York City. It was to house the world's largest amusement park and the world's largest ballroom. It was to host a circus, a roller-skating rink, a bowling alley, a theater, and the world's largest rotating restaurant.

It was the Globe Tower. And it was a fantastic long con.

In 1906 an advertisement appeared in the pages of the *New York Herald*. A developer named Samuel Friede was seeking investors for his ambitious Globe Tower project. He had acquired some land on Coney Island, next door to the popular Steeplechase amusement park.

Friede promised his investors a 100-percent return on their money *every year*. In retrospect that probably should have been every investor's first sign of trouble. But as we see over and over again with these stories, people wanted to believe that the dream of free money was possible. Friede, with the assistance of Edward Langan, a corrupt elevator inspector in Brooklyn, sold more than three hundred thousand dollars' worth of stock in the tower.

The groundbreaking ceremony was held in May 1906. There were speeches and fireworks and a concert. But strangely enough, nearly a year passed with no progress made on the site.

Investors got anxious, so Friede organized a *second* ceremony in early 1907. He announced plans to install eight hundred concrete pilings for

*Investors gave Samuel Friede their hard-earned cash and all they got was this lousy postcard.*

the tower's base. Each slab of concrete was thirty feet high and five feet around, which no doubt looked very impressive to the investors. Of course, nowadays, any good architect would question whether pilings that size could even support a building designed to hold fifty thousand people. And Friede never installed eight hundred pilings, anyway. The real number was closer to thirty.

Then everything fell apart. A man named Henry R. Wade, who had been the treasurer for the Globe project, was convicted on unrelated embezzlement charges. As part of his testimony, he confessed to a New York courtroom that the entire Globe Tower project had been a scam. Friede and Langan, as well as a couple of other coconspirators, had divided the three hundred thousand dollars between themselves and disappeared.

Wade was paid only four thousand dollars, and yet he was the only person involved to serve any jail time. The owner of Steeplechase Park was left with the problem of how to remove thirty useless concrete pilings from the property.

## Mon Dieu! Sacré Bleu!

Long cons require a keen understanding of human psychology. What do people want most, and what will they do to get it? As we've seen, many long cons are based primarily on human greed. But there are other, subtler desires that can also make people vulnerable to a skilled con man. Here's the story of one of the wildest long cons in recent memory.

Unlike the United States, European countries still have royalty kicking around. In some countries, royalty is still in power, but their power is mostly symbolic. For example, Queen Elizabeth II of England and King Felipe VI of Spain are officially heads of state, but aren't actively involved in politics. In other countries, royals have no power at all beyond their wealth and a generally accepted high social position. That's certainly true in France, a country that suffered years of bloody revolution before its royalty finally lost power. But despite all the heads that rolled, French aristocrats—upper-class families with large fortunes passed down over many generations—still exist in the twenty-first century.

Modern aristocrats tend to share a keen interest in their family history (or "line") and in the history of European aristocracy in general. And many seem to feel that they missed out on the "good old days," when being of "noble birth" granted more prestige than it does today. Unfortunately for one family of French aristocrats called the de Védrines, this longing for importance made them vulnerable to a con man.

About twenty years ago, in the late 1990s, a man named Thierry Tilly befriended Ghislaine de Védrines. Tilly claimed to be an investment expert, saying that he could steer the de Védrines family fortune into investments that would pay 10-percent interest per month. He also told Ghislaine that he was a descendant of the Hapsburgs—a detail that probably means nothing to you, but meant the world to Ghislaine. From the fifteenth to sixteenth centuries, the Hapsburgs were the most powerful royal family in Europe. Tilly also told Ghislaine that his grandmother was a friend of the former French president François Mitterrand and that his parents were an Olympic ice-skater and a combat swimmer, which is kind of like being a Navy SEAL, except French.

Once Tilly had won Ghislaine's trust, she introduced him to her husband, Jean, as well as her brother Charles-Henri and his wife, Christine, plus many other members of the de Védrines family. At that point, Tilly confided that he was actually a secret agent. He said that his boss, a shadowy member of Spanish royalty known only as "Gonzalez," had sent Tilly to protect the de Védrines from dark forces of a secretive group called the Freemasons.[14] According to Tilly, the Freemasons were after the de Védrines family's property and fortune, and they would happily kill to get it. Tilly also told them that the de Védrines line actually descended from another secret order, L'Équilibre du Monde (the Balance of the World), and that it was their destiny to save the world from the Freemasons.

The de Védrines family became so convinced of Tilly's story that they locked themselves away in their family château, abandoning jobs and even spouses to live together in secrecy with virtually no contact with the outside world. Tilly would not even allow them to have clocks or calendars. One family member later described Tilly as a "brain burglar," saying that he "opened their heads, took out their brains, and put in a new one."

Over the next few years, the de Védrines family turned over their entire fortune—totaling in the millions of euros—to Tilly. They also stopped paying taxes, which inspired the French government to confiscate most of their belongings. In 2007, family members fled to Oxford, England, where Tilly had relocated because of unrelated legal problems. The de Védrines took low-paying jobs at places like Burger King.[15] All the while, they were still convinced of their ultimate destiny as world-saving members of L'Équilibre du Monde.

---

[14] The Freemasons are a society that dates back to the Middle Ages and that—rightly or wrongly—tends to be the focus of a lot of conspiracy theories about how they supposedly control various governments and financial institutions.

[15] They were *having it Tilly's way*, apparently. (Rim shot!)

Tilly convinced some members of the family that Christine de Védrines was secretly hiding a vast treasure, held in a secret bank account somewhere in Brussels. So the other family members kidnapped Christine and tortured her for almost two weeks, trying to get her to reveal the totally nonexistent bank account number. Christine finally made up a fake number just to get the abuse to stop. But instead, they dragged her to Brussels. Christine had to go from bank to bank, asking if anyone recognized an account number *that she knew she'd invented*. Eventually she escaped her captors and reached the police, and Tilly's scheme began to unravel.

Police finally arrested him in Switzerland in 2009 and brought him back to France. After his 2012 trial that was a sensation in Europe, Tilly was convicted on charges of abuse and involuntary imprisonment. He loudly claimed he would appeal the verdict, on the grounds that he was a British citizen, not French, which was not true. After some legal wrangling in 2013, he was given a sentence of ten years.

The de Védrines family was left to pick up the pieces. So far, the vast majority of their fortune has never been found.

This gets to the heart of what's truly awful about long cons—the trail of wrecked lives they leave behind. Ghislaine wrote a book about the Tilly ordeal, which was adapted for French television. So she, at least, got something out of the experience. But the other family members suffered just as much and ended up with nothing. Ponzi's victims ended up poorer for having met him, while Madoff's clients were wiped out completely. The Albanians lost their money *and* their government, and all the Globe Tower investors got for their trouble was a bunch of ugly pilings that never turned into a building. It's almost—notice I say *almost!*—enough to take the fun out of *Fakers*. So next, let's explore some scams that don't hurt quite so much. Let's go to the carnival.

# CHAPTER 3

## Step Right Up! Carnivals and the Prince of Humbug

If you've ever been to a state fair, a music festival, or an amusement park, you've visited a midway. It's where you'll find food stalls, games like darts and Whac-A-Mole, and that smart aleck who claims he can guess your birthday just by looking at you. Back in the day, the circus midway was also where you would find the sideshow acts and the animal displays. The midway is where event organizers make the bulk of their profits. And for fakers of all stripes, the midway is where the action is.

### On the Midway: At Least the Fun Is Real

The first midway was created around 125 years ago, at the World's Columbian Exposition, also known as the Chicago World's Fair. (The word *Columbian* is in the name because the fair, which was held in 1893, celebrated the journey of Christopher Columbus to the New World.) More than 27 million people visited the fair, which took up almost seven hundred acres in the vicinity of Jackson Park in downtown Chicago. The World's Fair was the first to have a separate midway for amusements.[16]

---

[16] The site is now a city park, and it's still known to locals as "the Midway."

Many of the displays and attractions on the midway were produced by companies looking to make a profit. After enjoying financial success at the World's Fair, those companies began taking their shows on the road,

## INVENTING THE FUTURE AT THE WORLD'S FAIR

*World's Fair visitors stroll the midway.*

The midway at the Chicago World's Fair was pretty different from midways today. It had "ethnographic displays," which involved people from various world cultures dressed up in their traditional costumes. There was an Irish village, a Japanese bazaar, an Egyptian temple, and a Persian palace, among many others. For twenty-five cents, you could visit the International Dress and Costume Exhibit, aka the World Congress of Beauty, featuring "pretty girls and gorgeous costumes" from all around the globe. There was even a "Workingman's House," where you could see how a poor family in Philadelphia lived. (That exhibit was free.)

Supposedly these displays were educational, and no doubt some of them were. However, the presence of a large number of belly dancers suggests that visitors might have had other interests besides anthropology.

In addition to inventing the midway, the Chicago World's Fair introduced many other innovations. For example, Chicago had the very first Ferris wheel, because the people running the fair wanted to display something as cool as the Eiffel Tower, which had debuted at the World's Fair in Paris several years earlier. The Chicago fair was also where William Wrigley Jr. debuted his gum. And the first dishwasher was displayed at the fair by inventor Josephine Cochrane, who went on to found what would become the KitchenAid company.

often banding together to offer a few different spectacles at one time. The number of carnivals grew throughout the early twentieth century: according to the *St. James Encyclopedia of Popular Culture*, there were about three hundred traveling carnivals by the mid-1930s. Most of them included a sideshow, which featured performers like fire eaters and sword swallowers, along with "freaks" like a fat lady or a little person.

Some of these acts were (and are) real. There's no point in fake swallowing a sword, for example. And a little person is either very short or he isn't. But there are *plenty* of fakes at sideshows—although if you want to sound like you're "in the know," the carny term for fakes is *gaffs*. For instance, you can be pretty certain that "Spidora: Spider-Human Hybrid!" is going to turn out to be an attractive young lady in a spider costume. And actual "Siamese twins" (properly called *conjoined twins*) are extremely rare, so if you hear about a "double-bodied act" at a sideshow, it's probably a gaff, too. So-called Alligator People are usually made with green food dye. Bearded ladies are sometimes on the up-and-up, or they may be female impersonators. Fiji mermaids and jackalopes (rabbits with antlers) are simple taxidermy creations.

If you're like me, right now you're thinking, *Alligator People? Mermaids? Who comes up with this stuff?* Well, there's been a long line of fakers who have come up with this stuff, stretching back generations. Allow me to introduce you to the king, Mr. Phineas Taylor Barnum.

## The Prince of Humbug

P. T. Barnum is arguably the most famous faker there ever was. But he didn't much care for terms like *con* or *scam*. He argued that his shows were not defrauding anyone because they gave people exactly what they wanted—a little entertainment, a little mystery, a little excitement. And if the specific details of his shows weren't exactly true, well . . . *where's the harm?* For that reason, Barnum preferred the term *humbugs* to describe

the way he fooled the public. His ability to turn "humbugs" into entertainment and profit was unparalleled, and he found his greatest successes
in sideshows and, later, the circus.

Born in 1810 in Bethel, Connecticut, Barnum was an eager salesman
even as a kid. He was selling lottery tickets and rum by the time he was
twelve. At twenty-five, he got into the fakers business by organizing exhibitions for a woman named Joice Heth, who claimed to have been George
Washington's nurse.[17]

The Heth experience whetted Barnum's appetite for creating shows.
In 1842 his sense of showmanship combined with his business acumen
in the creation of the American Museum in New York City. At its height
the American Museum had about 850,000 exhibits, including paintings,
wax figures, and insect collections. There were taxidermy animal displays
and real animals on view as well, including lions, tigers, hippos, monkeys,
kangaroos, and even several whales in giant tanks down in the basement.
Still, among the real exhibits, there was plenty of fakery.

For example, in 1842 Barnum leased "the Fiji mermaid" from a man
named Moses Kimball. The supposed mermaid was about eighteen inches
long, with sharp teeth and a fish tail. It was said to have been discovered
by Japanese sailors years earlier. In truth the Fiji mermaid was a monkey
head attached to a dead fish . . . but that was good enough for Barnum.
He invented a new story about the mermaid having been found in South
America and "leaked" the information to New York papers to whip up
interest in the creature.[18]

Barnum didn't limit himself to mere displays. There were frequent
shows and lectures held at the museum—everything from glassblowing

---

[17] Heth was quite a faker in her own right; you can find her story in chapter 5.

[18] The Fiji mermaid's popularity endures! You can still find versions of her in "museums of the weird" such
as the Ripley's Believe It or Not! chain. Some Fiji mermaids are actually devilfish, which are a type of ray,
similar to a manta ray. Other "mermaids" kick it old-school with the monkey/fish routine.

and sewing-machine demonstrations to concerts and plays. There were also special events, such as flower shows, bird shows, and even, in 1843, the Grand Buffalo Hunt. The "hunt" itself was held at a racetrack in Hoboken, New Jersey. The buffalo were all young and slow, and they weren't actually hunted, just chased around a bit and then caught with a lasso. Audiences weren't angry at the misrepresentation because it was a nice day out, there was a band playing, and everybody went home happy. In that sense, the Grand Buffalo Hunt was the perfect encapsulation of Barnum's no-harm-no-foul vision of a "humbug."[19]

*An advertisement for Barnum's so-called "Wonderful Albino Family," who were displayed at the museum beginning in 1857. Barnum claimed that their family name was Eliophobus and that they were from Madagascar. But, in fact, Rudolph and Antoinette Lucasie were from somewhere in Europe (possibly France).*

The museum also hosted a regular event called the Grand National Baby Show, where you could see the "finest babies" in various categories: finest baby under one year, fattest baby, handsomest twins, and so on. There were prizes for runners-up as well; imagine the disappointment of being declared "third-finest baby"! Still, audiences loved it.

In his autobiography, Barnum recalls how the museum became so popular that the building would fill up very early in the day. Alas, visitors would stay far too long—even bringing their lunches so that they could spend the entire day at the museum. That left hundreds of people outside on the street, unable to get inside. In other words, people wanted to give

---

[19] If you think Barnum was having a sudden fit of generosity, think again: Barnum made a substantial profit by renting out boats that ferried people from Manhattan across the river to the racetrack.

*This portrait of Charles Stratton exaggerates his height. Yes, Stratton was small; no, he was not pocket-sized, as suggested here.*

Barnum their money but were unable to—this simply could not be allowed! To, let's say, *encourage* more people to leave, Barnum had a sign painted in giant letters that said TO THE EGRESS, with a big arrow. Eager visitors would stream through the door, mistakenly believing that an egress must be some new animal they'd never seen before.[20]

Barnum also organized tours for different types of performers, such as a singer named Jenny Lind, who became known as the Swedish Nightingale. He made a celebrity out of Charles Stratton, better known as General Tom Thumb. As a child, Stratton was roughly two feet tall; he eventually grew to reach a bit over three feet. Barnum routinely advertised Stratton as being somewhat older and somewhat smaller than reality. General Tom Thumb toured America and all across Europe, even meeting with royalty. It seemed, for a time, that everything Barnum touched turned into giant piles of cash.

Then in 1865 the entire American Museum burned to the ground. Although the roof collapsed and a great many of the animals died, no people were killed. However, firefighters accidentally rescued Barnum's collection of wax figures, which they dragged out of the burning building

---

[20] It wasn't. The word *egress* just means "exit." D'oh!

## DUELING GIANTS

In 1869 George Hull got into an argument about the Bible. A Methodist reverend argued that the line "There were giants in the earth" (Genesis 6:4) proved that giants really existed. Hull thought this was ridiculous.

To mock the reverend, Hull hired stonemasons to carve a ten-foot giant from a soft, chalk-like material called gypsum. Hull buried the giant in the yard of William Newell, a tobacco farmer in Cardiff, New York. Then Newell excitedly reported that he "discovered" this amazing thing while trying to dig a well.

The Cardiff Giant caused a sensation. Soon it was taken to Syracuse, New York, and people traveled from great distances to see it. And when an expert from Yale University examined the statue and declared it a fake? People nicknamed the giant Old Hoaxey and kept lining up anyway.

P. T. Barnum asked to rent the giant for his American Museum, but the owners refused. So Barnum made his *own* Cardiff Giant and displayed that instead. Old Hoaxey's owners then sued Barnum for stealing their idea. But the judge declared that for the case to go forward, the gentlemen from Syracuse would need to prove that *their* Cardiff Giant was authentic. The owners promptly dropped their suit.

Today, the original (fake) Cardiff Giant is on display in Cooperstown, New York, and Barnum's fake (fake) Cardiff Giant is at Marvin's Marvelous Mechanical Museum, near Detroit.

thinking they were human. The cause of the fire has never been determined for certain. Historians suspect that it was set deliberately, possibly by Confederate loyalists.[21] This has never been proven. Barnum went on to open a new museum, and that, too, burned to the ground in 1868.

After that, Barnum went into politics—he represented Connecticut in Congress from 1865 to 1869, and then he was briefly mayor of the city

---

[21] The eight-man Confederate Army of Manhattan set fire to the museum in 1864 as part of a wider plot to burn down New York City. Their leader, Robert Cobb Kennedy, was executed at the close of the war.

of Bridgeport from 1875 to 1876. But the Prince of Humbug was not quite done with the midway. Barnum created his first circus in 1871, and he recruited many of his old comrades from the American Museum days. The show was called P. T. Barnum's Grand Traveling Museum, Menagerie, Caravan, and Circus. Throughout numerous mergers and many name changes, the circus spent decades on the road, bringing entertainment to hundreds of millions of kids and adults until it was finally shut down for good in 2017.

## Carnival Games

Years ago carnival games were rigged to fleece suckers as efficiently as possible. But around the 1970s, the public's association of carnivals with rip-offs got to be really bad for business—and caused endless hassles with local police officers. Nowadays carnival games are not fake . . . or, not exactly. I mean, you *can* win games . . . *maybe*. But that isn't to say that carnies don't bend the rules a bit.

So in the interest of improving your next trip to the midway, here's the inside scoop on some of the most popular carnival games.

*Darts.* It's pretty rare that you'll see a midway that doesn't have at least one darts game. Sometimes the player has to throw a dart at balloons; other times the player has to aim at little red stars like bull's-eyes. These games aren't fake: if you break the balloon or hit the star, you really will win something. But carnies have a few techniques for making victory as challenging as possible: the darts are of low quality and the tips are dull, which makes it hard to burst a balloon. The darts might be either lighter or heavier than usual darts, in order to throw off the aim of experienced darts players. Ironically the better you are at actual darts, the worse you'll do at carnival darts. If you've already trained yourself on how darts *should* behave in the air, carnival darts won't do what you expect.

Another technique involves underinflating the balloons, which makes them less likely to burst. They are also attached to the board very lightly, meaning that the slightest breeze—say, from a dart flying through the air!—can cause them to abruptly change position.

Carnies have also been known to monkey around with other tar-

> *"If it looks easy, it isn't. If it looks impossible, it just might be. If looks like fun—hey, that's what the carnival is all about."*
> —Bret Witter, **Carnival Undercover**

gets. For example, while the stars might look like bright, beautiful bull's-eyes, look again. The "arms" of the star make it look bigger, but that space is actually very narrow and extremely hard to hit. Meanwhile the center of the star is smaller than a typical bull's-eye.

But if you're determined to play this game, take a tip from Bret Witter, author of *Carnival Undercover*: the best prizes are usually behind the balloons at the upper part of the board. Those are the hardest balloons to break, as most people's darts end up on the board's lower half. So if you're going to aim, aim high.

*Ringtoss.* The ringtoss is one of the oldest and trickiest games on the midway. The rings are so light that even when they hit one of the bottles, they tend to bounce off again. That's why Witter recommends the "ricochet" method: he says to throw the ring like a Frisbee and skim it, as though you are skimming rocks, across the surface of the bottles. That way, the ring is less likely to bounce away erratically and more likely to come to rest gently atop one of the bottles.

*Ball Toss.* There are lots of variations on this game, including throwing a softball at milk bottles, a Wiffle ball into a basket, or a Ping-Pong ball into a goldfish bowl. Ball-toss games are carnival classics, and they all work the same way: throw the first thing into the second thing, in order to win the third thing. Couldn't be simpler, right?

Well . . . carnies have a few tricks to make these "simple" games harder than they might appear. Sometimes they use optical illusions. For instance, have you ever seen that game where you throw a softball into giant milk cans? Standing on the midway, it looks like you have a massive target, but that's an illusion: most milk-can openings are actually only 1/16 of an inch wider than a softball.

Or maybe you've tried to use that softball to knock over some milk bottles.[22] It might look easy, but those bottles are made to be heavier than you think. Some of them are even made of lead! Good luck knocking *those* over.

Then there's the game where you throw a wiffle ball or a basketball into a basket. Unlike the milk cans, the baskets are obviously quite wide, so it should be easy, right? Well, this time the trick has to do with the angle of the basket. Again, there is a visual illusion that makes you think you know the best angle, but you really don't. Carnies also sometimes hang prizes right over the basket or use a lot of visually confusing signs behind them to throw off your aim.

The easiest of the lot tends to be throwing the ping-pong ball into the goldfish bowl. In that case, you have water tension on your side—when the light ping-pong ball hits the water, the water tension will often help keep the ball in place. In this instance, the only trick involved is that goldfish only cost about ten cents apiece, but you paid a dollar to win one.

The value of the goldfish brings me to the most important thing to understand about carnival games: the value of the prize (or lack thereof). Even when games aren't faked at all—even if the darts are sharp, the softballs are weighted correctly, and everything is completely aboveboard—the prizes always cost substantially less than the amount you paid to play. And when I say substantially, I mean ten cents on the dollar or even less. In effect even when you win—even if *everybody* wins—the carny already made his profit anyway.

---

[22] I know what you're thinking: What is it with carnies and milk? It's just tradition. Back in the day, milk cans and bottles were easy to get ahold of.

*The knockdown game, as this is sometimes called, is fun but likely rigged—the cans on the bottom row are probably much heavier than they appear.*

What about the giant prizes, like those stuffed animals that are the size of your little brother? You always see some lucky person lugging one around on the midway . . . surely those are worth more than the price of the game. Right?

Well, yeah, they might be. Two things to understand, though: First, winning the giant prizes almost always involves playing the same game multiple times and "stepping up" the prize over and over. First you win, I don't know, a comb or something. Then you move up to the key chain, then the tiny stuffed animal, and so on. The person you see carrying that giant panda might have paid quite a lot in order to win it—far more than it's worth.

But here's one more secret: the person carrying around the panda might not have won it at all. Carnies routinely pay someone to simply *carry the prize around*, in order to tempt other people on the midway.

## Guessing Games

Another grand old tradition on the midway is the carny who claims to know more about you than a stranger ever could. For a fee, the "guesser," as this job is called, will predict your age, weight, or birthday. Usually the guesser writes the number down on a piece of paper, and if the number is correct—usually within a range, like two years for age or ten pounds for weight—you lose. But if you fool the guesser, you win a prize.

How do they do it? When it comes to guessing weight and age, with enough practice, a person can learn to size others up pretty well, just with visual cues. Guessers look for physical signs of age, for example, like wrinkles or bald spots. They also glance at the people *with* the person, assuming that their friends or family might provide a clue. Experienced weight and age guessers are also aware that people can look prematurely aged. So for instance, if a man takes off his hat to make sure the guesser notices that he has gray hair, the guesser will probably guess younger than expected—because he is a carny, and he knows when he's being played.

None of this is magic; mostly it's just a matter of instinct and practice. That said, some guessers do cheat. One method is to quickly write down two different numbers and show you only the one that's the most accurate. So for example a guesser might look at a young woman and scribble down the numbers nineteen and twenty-five. If she says she's twenty-four, the guesser will only show the paper where he wrote twenty-five; he won't show the guess that was way off.

But what about birthdays? How can you know people's birthdays just by looking at them? Well, you can't, obviously—this is an old trick.

First of all, the rules of the game often specify that the guesser only

has to get within two months of the actual birth month. So if your birthday is in June, the guesser can say anywhere from April to August and still be considered "right." That's five out of twelve months, or almost fifty-fifty odds before the game even begins! Even guessers who only give themselves a window of one month on either side still have a one in four chance.

And again, there is sometimes a bit of shenanigans with that piece of paper. Some guessers write with deliberately bad handwriting, creating a scribble that could arguably read "January" or "July." That improves the guesser's odds even more.

Finally, as I mentioned earlier, the prize that the person wins cost only about a quarter of whatever the person paid to play the game. So whether you're throwing darts or letting someone guess your birthday, the key is to do it for fun, rather than any sort of profit. P. T. Barnum, the great-granddaddy of the midway, understood this all too well. Sometimes we know, deep down, that we are being fooled—but we don't really mind, because we appreciate the experience itself.

# CHAPTER 4

## Mysterious Minds: Spoon Benders and Psychics

Just a generation ago, a carnival wasn't really a carnival if it didn't have a psychic, palm reader, or some other type of fortune-teller as part of the entertainment. Psychics are far less common at carnivals these days, but that doesn't mean they've gone away. Far from it! The "psychic services industry" earns roughly two billion dollars every year. Some psychics operate out of their own storefronts, while others reach customers through call-in lines or the Internet. Some enterprising psychics sell their services on websites like Etsy. There are even "psychic fairs," where visitors can sample a whole host of hoodoo at once.

Now, far be it from me to suggest that you shouldn't follow your horoscope, get your palm read, or even try to contact a long-dead relative if you are in the mood to do so. But as the great skeptic James Randi supposedly said, "There is a distinct difference between having an open mind and having a hole in your head from which your brain leaks out."

## Bending Minds and Flatware

Uri Geller is an Israeli immigrant who became famous in the 1970s for the ability to bend metal and repair watches with his mind. In 1973 Geller was scheduled to make a major appearance on *The Tonight Show*. But in advance of the show, producers contacted James Randi, a famous critic of psychics, for advice about how to set up the interview. At Randi's suggestion, the host presented Geller with spoons and other objects, to see whether Geller could bend them. But Randi also advised the host that Geller should not be allowed to touch the spoons before the interview. Asked to perform under these conditions, Geller failed completely. He

## THE AMAZING RANDI

*James Randi in 2007.*

Born in 1928 in Toronto, Canada, the man who would become known as James Randi spent much of his childhood attending magic shows rather than school. He left home at age seventeen to join a carnival as a magician. Randi became an expert magician, but it was important to him that audiences always understand he was performing tricks, not *actual* magic. He believed strongly that sleight of hand and other techniques should be used only to entertain, never to deceive. He was furious at people who used basic conjuring tricks to fool others into believing they had ESP or could contact the dead. And so Randi began a second career as a professional skeptic.

In 1964 he offered a one-thousand-dollar reward to anyone who could demonstrate psychic ability under scientific conditions. No one was able to claim the award that year, or the next year, or the next. Randi has offered the prize every year since. He has even raised the reward to one million dollars. Many would-be psychics have attempted Randi's Million Dollar Challenge, but every single one has failed.[23]

---

[23] Randi is the subject of a fascinating documentary called *An Honest Liar* (2014).

was humiliated. Years later he would tell an interviewer that he fully assumed his career was over after that experience.

> *"I am a liar, a cheat, and a charlatan."*
> —*James Randi, in the traditional opening to his magic shows*

But just the opposite occurred. Many people who saw the show decided that if Geller were able to perform on command every time, this would suggest that it was all just a trick and easily repeated. The fact that Geller could not perform on *The Tonight Show* was taken, strangely enough, as evidence that his gifts were real!

And so began a rivalry between Randi and Geller that would last for many years. Randi published a lengthy exposé called *The Truth About Uri Geller* in 1982. In response, Geller sued Randi and his publisher not once but three separate times. (All the lawsuits were thrown out.) The pair even appeared together from time to time, clashing over whether Geller's "abilities" were supernatural in nature. Geller took to referring to Randi as "my most influential and important publicist."

Geller's star has waned in recent years. In 2013 he appeared in a TV show called *The Secret Life of Uri Geller* on Britain's BBC. He claimed that he had been employed as a "psychic spy" by the Central Intelligence Agency, and that he had used his mental powers to erase computer disks of Russia's KGB.

## So...How Do They Do It?

In one corner we have Uri Geller, master psychic and bender of spoons, keys, and other metal objects. In the other corner we have James Randi, noted skeptic who assures us this is all just a trick. All right, then: if it's a trick, how does it work?

There are actually several ways to accomplish the illusion of bending a spoon, most of which involve sleight of hand. If you pick up a spoon and stroke the neck, you can make it look like you're gradually forcing

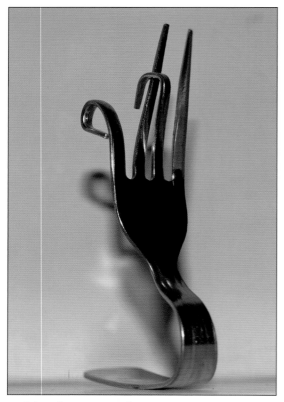

*Fork bent by James Randi.*

the spoon to bend—but actually you used your thumb to bend the spoon when you first picked it up. You can also do this with the tine of a fork by flicking the fork very quickly in the air. The flicking motion is to hide the fact that you actually bent the tine with your fingers as you picked it up. Another sleight-of-hand method is to use spoons that are already broken and hide that fact from your audience, so it appears that you, the psychic, have caused the breaks.

A third method is even easier, and it relies on a simple optical illusion. Hold the spoon straight up and down, with the bottom of the bowl part facing a hard surface and both your hands stacked and wrapped around the handle so the handle is not visible. Then press the bottom of the bowl part down against the surface of the table. Let the handle move toward your body, but keep your hands straight. This will make the spoon appear to bend. But what's really going on is that you are holding your top hand straight as you "bend" the spoon. It will look like the handle is curving, but your hands are hiding the fact that you are actually just holding the spoon at an angle. Then you gradually "unbend" the spoon by slowly straightening the angle of your hands. If you're having trouble picturing this trick, just search online for "how to bend spoons," and all will be revealed.

As James Randi famously said, "If Uri Geller bends spoons with divine powers, then he's doing it the hard way."

## Thoroughly Modern Mitchells

Picture a sophisticated city like New York. You figure people have to be pretty street-smart to live there. Now think about a part of New York City called the West Village, which has a long association with highly artistic, educated, sophisticated people. Not to mention *wealthy* people. West Village real estate is among the most expensive in the entire United States. And yet, in her small West Village storefront, Zena the Clairvoyant fleeced her sophisticated clientele for *years* before she was finally arrested.

Zena's real name is Sylvia Mitchell. You won't find her on Bleecker Street anymore. But not so long ago, she was apparently making a fine living thanks to clients like Lee Choong. Choong was an investment banker who was unsatisfied with her career and her romantic life, and she was also extremely worried about her sick mother. In that vulnerable frame of mind, Choong visited Zena for a reading in 2007. Zena informed Choong that her "energy field" was in trouble, but that it could be fixed. The first step was for Choong to give Zena eighteen thousand dollars to keep in a jar. Zena explained that putting the money in a jar was simply a spiritual "exercise"—Choong could get the money back anytime.[24]

Zena revealed that Choong's troubles all stemmed from unresolved problems from a past life. Those problems could be fixed, but it would take time, many visits, and large amounts of costly "supplies." Over the next two years, Choong forked over an astounding 128 thousand dollars to Zena. Choong ended up losing her job as well as all her money.

Eventually Choong banded together with another woman who had also been swindled by Zena. Debra Saalfield had surrendered twenty-seven thousand dollars to Zena's magical jar, also to fix problems in a past life. But Saalfield had second thoughts and tried to get the money back right away. When she couldn't, Saalfield went to the police. This eventu-

---

[24] Spoiler alert: No. No, she couldn't.

ally led to Mitchell's 2013 conviction for multiple counts of grand larceny. As one of the jurors told a reporter, "She was clearly robbing these people in a heinous way."

Mitchell is not the only New York psychic convicted of fraud in the past few years. Amazingly, she isn't even the only person named *Mitchell* convicted of fraud in the past few years! Another fake psychic from New York, also named Sylvia Mitchell, confessed in a parole hearing that the fortune-telling racket is "just corruption." And in yet another New York hearing, this one in 2014, a *different* Mitchell, called Celia, was asked, "What is the psychic business? Is it real, or a bunch of baloney?" Celia Mitchell's answer: "It's a scam, sir."

I can offer no explanation for the number of psychic Mitchells in the New York prison system. There is no evidence that they are related. But not all psychics are named Mitchell, and as you'll soon learn, not all their victims are women.

## Cold as Ice: Psychics and Mediums

How do psychics seem to know your life without having met you before? How do spiritualists know just what people want to hear from their great-grandmothers beyond the grave? Do some people really have a special talent for seeing the future or talking to the dead? Sure, they have a talent, all right. But it's not the one they claim to have.

Whether the props involve a crystal ball, a deck of cards, or the palm of someone's hand, these types of psychic performances boil down to a technique called cold reading. Cold reading involves figuring out information about strangers based solely on looking at them and talking to them. A journalist named Tony Ortega explained cold reading this way: "[It's] a skill that does not require any kind of supernatural element. It's just a skill that uses a good understanding of human nature and a good understanding of what your subjects want."

## GETTING AWAY WITH IT

It is incredible to consider that Sylvia Mitchell, a pretty obvious con artist, had a storefront right in the middle of New York City for years. Sometimes people refer to criminals as "hiding in plain sight," but it's hard to argue that Mitchell was hiding at all!

How do scammers get away with this stuff?

Well, we've already discussed how badly we all want to believe that we are special and that what looks "too good to be true" will actually be true for us. When it comes to cons like Mitchell's, we shouldn't overlook the power of another emotion: shame. Yes, cases like Saalfield's and Choong's are both extreme and extremely embarrassing. However, *many* people get taken for smaller amounts of money. They never report it because they feel foolish. They fear others will think they're foolish, too. As Saalfield put it, being scammed by Zena the Clairvoyant was "one of the most humiliating things that's ever happened to me." In an odd way, the victims of con artists end up being recruited as their greatest protectors.

We all "read" one another constantly. What we're wearing, how we move, who we're with, the unintentional expressions on our faces—all these factors and hundreds of others provide tiny clues about us, even before we speak. And once we do get talking, we give up even more information, often without realizing it. Learning how to read cues from others is an important skill for humans to have. The problem starts when people use that skill to cheat one another. Fake psychics fish for information from their clients and then pretend that the information came from some supernatural source.

One cold-reading technique is the leading question. For example, a psychic might say something like, "I'm sensing the letter *J*. Does that mean anything to you?" And the customer says, "Yes, my dead father's name was John!" Interestingly when the customer tells friends about the experience

> "I can spot someone's weakness a mile away.
> In any room I can pick out the best target.
> . . . Ultimately, anyone can be conned."
> —Simon Lovell, former cardshark,
> in a 2008 interview

later, he is likely to say something like, "The psychic knew that my father's name was John." But that's not really what happened. The psychic asked an open-ended question, and the customer provided the information.

Another technique involves making a vague statement and then watching the body language of the listener. If the customer makes a face like he disagrees, then the reader quickly makes the opposite statement. For example, the reader might say, "Your dead father, John, seems unhappy. . . ." If the listener nods even a tiny bit, the reader knows to proceed along the "unhappiness" track. But if the customer's eyebrows furrow together in confusion, the reader will quickly say, "Which is strange, because he was so happy normally." And then the reading goes on.

A magician and professional skeptic known as Penn Jillette compared cold readings to playing charades. What he meant was, the psychic is basically saying, "Sounds like . . . shoe? Blue? New? Oh, *new!* Of course, I see something *new.*"

The great showman P. T. Barnum[25] observed that people want to be fooled so badly that they will actually *help* you fool them. If you make a general statement (sometimes called a "Barnum statement"), people will tend to figure out how that statement applies to them. This creates the illusion that the person who made the statement understands the stranger, but it's not true. The statement was just very general, and the reality is that almost all people worry about almost all the same stuff.

If I say, *One thing I know about you, dear reader, is that you sometimes worry that you aren't good enough.* You might think, "Wow, this writer

---

[25] If you missed it, you can read all about Barnum in chapter 3. (Dude! Why'd you skip chapter 3?)

really knows me." But in fact all I know is that pretty much everybody feels that way sometimes! Or here's another example. *I am having a vision right now, and I see you, dear reader, arguing with an older person.* But wait, how could I know that you argued with your parents recently? Well, I didn't! But who hasn't argued with a parent, a teacher, or some other authority figure at some point?

This is sometimes called subjective validation. That's a term for the tendency humans have to place specific personal meanings on general statements. It's sometimes called the Forer effect, due to the work of a psychologist named Bertram Forer. In a famous 1948 experiment, he gave a personality test to a group of his students. He told the students that he'd use their answers to give them specific reports about their personalities. Instead, he ignored their answers and gave them all the exact same report. Despite this, the vast majority of the students felt that the personality report was accurate and specific to them.

If we can connect with a statement—like if you read my statement above and immediately thought of an argument you had with an older

## MONSTERS OF THE MIDWAY

In his book *Monster Midway* (1953), William Lindsay Gresham passed along what he'd learned during his time with a traveling carnival. According to him, a good cold reader understands that "people fall into a few basic categories, that their lives are pretty much the same."

With this insight, Gresham breaks people down into various categories, noting that you can usually tell what the person wants to hear simply by looking at them. For instance, if a young man looks "flashy," he is worried about a girl—either he can't get one or he can't get rid of one. But if he looks like the serious type, he's worried about his career.

The world has changed a lot since Gresham's day. But his basic observation does make sense—we aren't as distinctive as we like to think. And armed with this understanding, con artists can get into our heads pretty easily.

person—then it's a natural human tendency to assume that the statement is correct. Subjective validation makes extremely general things feel very personal.

I might be making cold reading sound quite easy, but a good cold reading—the kind that can convince a person that their mind has been read—can be tricky. So sometimes con men try and tip the scales by doing something called a hot reading. A hot reading is one where the performer has secretly gathered information about the person ahead of time. For instance, in 1986, the magician and skeptic James Randi (discussed earlier in this chapter) exposed a televangelist named Peter Popoff. Popoff would shock and amaze his audiences by the way he appeared to know everything about them—from their medical conditions to their home addresses. The televangelist claimed he knew so much because God spoke to him directly. Randi proved that it wasn't God providing Popoff the information, but rather Popoff's wife, who had gathered the information beforehand and conveyed it to her husband via a tiny radio receiver in Popoff's ear.

But if the psychic is truly skilled, a hot reading isn't necessary. You'd be amazed at how much information people give away without even opening their mouths.

## Fool for Love

*Think of a person going through difficult times. Perhaps it's a death in the family, addiction, they could have just been let go from their job, even an illness or physical injury. Each one of those people you are thinking of has the potential to be a future victim of this crime.*

These words were written by Niall Rice, and he would know: he lost more than half a million dollars to a Times Square psychic named Priscilla Kelly Delmaro.

In 2013 Rice was living in Brooklyn, New York. He had just returned from a stint in a drug rehab program in Arizona. While there, he'd developed a crush on a woman named Michelle. She made it clear she wasn't interested, but Rice couldn't let it go. He eventually ended up at Delmaro's psychic storefront on West Forty-Third Street. She assured Rice that he and Michelle were destined to be together; she offered to communicate with the spirit world and get him some help from the other side. The first visit cost Rice twenty-five hundred dollars; the second cost nine thousand dollars. But that was just the beginning.

Delmaro convinced Rice to buy a forty-thousand-dollar diamond ring—the diamond had something to do with improving Rice's psychic energy, and as a bonus he could eventually give it to Michelle as an engagement ring.[26] On Delmaro's advice, Rice visited Michelle, who had moved to California, but things didn't go well. Michelle thought Rice was "acting weird."

---

[26] Psst: That never happened.

But Rice was hooked at this point, and he paid more and more. Delmaro told him she needed eighty thousand dollars to build an eighty-mile gold bridge in "the other realm" in order to lure a spirit across. But the Golden Bridge Project apparently suffered some cost overruns; more money was needed to build a second bridge, ten miles longer than the first. For another fee, Delmaro offered to acquire a time machine to go back and fix Rice's spiritual problems at their root.

When Rice discovered that Michelle had died, it seemed that hope was lost. But Delmaro assured Rice that death was no obstacle. She could simply inject Michelle's spirit into a different woman's body.

## PSYCHICS ONLINE

If you're out on Venice Beach in California or in Jackson Square in New Orleans, you might choose to drop a little cash on the many tarot-card readers who hang out there. Even if you know it isn't real, talking to a "psychic" can still be fun. As long as you remember that you're being "cold read" rather than "mind read," there's usually no harm done.

*However* (you knew there was a however, didn't you?), it's important to be very careful about any kind of *online* psychic. Remember "hot readings"? Online psychics give the hottest of hot readings. Think about it—you can't see the person, so you don't know what he or she is doing. An online psychic can perform an extensive Internet search on a customer without the customer having any idea what's going on.

We all leave online trails of personal information. Having access to something as simple as an email can eventually turn up all kinds of data that you probably thought was private.

Bob Nygaard, an investigator who specializes in psychic fraud, issued a strong warning about online psychics. "They're going online for public records and seeing what kind of property people own," he told one reporter, "how much they have, if they're worth it, if they're a good mark." Fake psychics can use the power of the Internet to turn a supposedly harmless reading into full-blown identity theft.

Rice flew back out to California to meet "new Michelle," but she didn't fit the description that Delmaro had given him at all. Rice later said that it was this fact—the mismatch between the woman he'd been promised and the one he met—that "caused [him] to start thinking that Delmaro wasn't everything she was purporting to be." That's what did it. Not, you know, the time machine.

Rice finally went to the police. He told a detective that Delmaro had taken him for $713,975. She was arrested and eventually convicted of grand larceny, just like Sylvia Mitchell.

But this amazing story doesn't end there. It came out that the real amount that Delmaro had taken from Rice—the amount Delmaro confessed to in court—was $557,441. Not $713,975, as he originally stated. The additional money? Rice had given that to *a totally different psychic*. While it doesn't fundamentally change Delmaro's crimes, the fact that Rice hadn't been honest made a huge mess for the prosecution.

Another complicating factor was the fact that Rice and Delmaro became romantically involved in the middle of the scam. It is pretty common for con artists to start romances with their marks, because it makes fraud cases more difficult to prosecute. Delmaro's attorney argued that the "relationship" was much different from what Rice claimed.

In the end, Delmaro served only eight months in jail and was released on probation. Delmaro's attorney assured reporters that "she won't be a psychic anymore."

## CHAPTER 5

### Who Are You? Impostors

In researching this book, I plucked for you a big, beautiful bouquet of fakers: from street hustlers to Nigerian emailers, from sideshow carnies to Ponzi schemers. But of all the many types of fakers, the slipperiest tend to be the impostors.

A short-con artist will lie to you for a few minutes. A long-con artist might lie to you for weeks or months. A carnie will give you a "prize" that's worth a tenth of what you paid for it. They'll all take your money, and they'll all probably take your trust. But an impostor is something else again. The impostor strikes at the very notion of identity, asking us to wonder whether we ever truly know anyone. And whether anyone can ever really know us.

There are fakers all over the world, but the United States seems to be a particularly fertile territory for the impostor. The pursuit of happiness, not to mention the pursuit of cash, is what impostors are all about. After all it's pretty rare for impostors to pretend to be poorer than they are in real life! Living in "the land of opportunity" seems to inspire people to remake themselves, even at the expense of the truth.

## She *Could* Tell a Lie. . . .

Before P. T. Barnum was a world-famous impresario, he was just an ambitious young man from Connecticut. One day he saw a show that featured an elderly enslaved woman named Joice Heth. Heth was "owned" at the time by event promoter R. W. Lindsay, and her act involved pretending to be the childhood nurse of George Washington. She *did* look quite old, it's true—but she would have had to have been more than 160 for her claims to be accurate. But Heth put on a good show, spinning stories about the childhood of "young George" and nimbly answering every question the audience asked about our Founding Father.

The problem was, Heth's audiences were quite small. Lindsay wasn't able to convince audiences that they should be interested. Barnum knew he could do better.

He sold his share in a grocery business to get the one thousand dollars to purchase Heth's show. As her new promoter, he then wrote (or had written) a pamphlet called "The Life of Joice Heth," which laid out her fake biography in detail. Barnum understood that seeing a story printed in an official-looking document would have a greater impact than just hearing about it. The pamphlet claimed that Heth was born in Madagascar in 1674, captured by a cruel slave trader, and later "rescued" by the Washington family.[27]

Barnum set up exhibitions for Heth in major cities across the country. He then manipulated the local media to drum up interest in her performance. In each town he hired doctors or other "experts" to examine Heth

---

[27] Not a word of this story was true. It was nonsense, balderdash, and to use Barnum's favorite term, humbug.

*A poster advertises Joice Heth, who was not really born in Madagascar, not really George Washington's nurse, and not nearly as old as she claimed.*

in advance of the show. But here's where Barnum's genius shined through: he didn't hire doctors to vouch for Heth. Instead, he got some to say she was legitimate and others to claim she was a fake. Barnum would then encourage both sides to fight it out in the pages of local newspapers. Whether or not Heth was real wasn't really the point. *Controversy*, Barnum knew, was what sold tickets—not facts.

At one point, antislavery activists in Providence, Rhode Island, objected to the show. They argued that Heth was still enslaved and that paying to see her show was making money only for her owner, not her. So Barnum planted a story about how the proceeds from Heth's performances were actually going into a fund to free her grandchildren from slavery. But the majority of that "fund" presumably stayed right where Barnum believed it belonged—in his pocket.[28]

Eventually audiences got bored with Heth's act. So Barnum's assistant Levi Lyman published an editorial claiming not only that Heth was a fraud, but that she was not even human! The piece argued that Heth was actually an automaton made of rubber. Audiences flocked back to the show, wanting to decide for themselves whether she was human or not.

Heth died in 1836, but Barnum wasn't finished. He hired one of New York City's most respected doctors to perform a public autopsy. More than a thousand people paid fifty cents apiece to watch. The doctor declared Heth to be a fraud, saying she was only about eighty years old. But even that didn't really settle the matter. Barnum told the *New York Herald* that her death itself was faked—and that the autopsied body wasn't Heth's body at all but a stand-in. He later took that back as well.

Barnum never revealed the whole truth about Heth. At certain points he claimed that he had invented the act and taught Heth what to say and

---

[28] We have only Barnum's word regarding the details of his arrangement with Heth, and he changed his story numerous times. Because Barnum was the very definition of what English teachers call "an unreliable narrator," we can't say with certainty how much Heth might have profited, if at all.

do. At other points he claimed the hoax was entirely her idea and that he had been fooled along with everyone else. The truth probably lies somewhere in the middle.

Unfortunately this fog of lies makes us unable to determine very much about the real Heth and her actual biography. But one thing we do know for sure is that Heth was performing her "Washington's Nurse" act long before Barnum came along. There's no doubt that Barnum turned Heth into a celebrity. But any claims that *her* act was his idea are—you guessed it—fake.

## Lifestyles of the Relatives of the Rich and Famous

Joice Heth built a false identity, re-creating herself as a sort of celebrity-once-removed, and then she turned that identity into a show. She's far from the only person to pretend to be a friend or family member of a celebrity—although most impostors don't get up on stage and invite people to interview them! Most of the time impostors have some other goal in mind; frequently, it's one that can be measured in dollar signs.

Canadian-born Elizabeth Bigley was just thirteen years old in 1870, when she was arrested for her first check-cashing fraud. She'd forged a letter claiming that a relative had died and that she would be receiving an inheritance. She then convinced a bank to allow her to write checks on the (nonexistent) money. Bigley was caught within a few months and swore she'd never run that scam again. But she ended up returning to the same basic con over and over again throughout her life.

It was a life of multiple scams, aliases, and forgeries, but her greatest dubious achievement took place in 1902. Living in Ohio under the alias Cassie L. Chadwick, she began claiming that she was a "lost Carnegie"—the secret daughter of mega-rich businessman Andrew Carnegie.[29] As an

---

[29] Carnegie began life as a poor immigrant from Scotland but eventually sold his company, Carnegie Steel, for $480 million, or about $370 billion in modern dollars.

adult, Chadwick's schemes were more ambitious than her childhood cons, but ultimately it all boiled down to that same scam she'd pulled in 1870. She would use forged documents to convince bank managers that she was a Carnegie. Believing that she was an heir to massive wealth, banks were willing to give her similarly massive loans. And Chadwick used that money to fund a lifestyle every bit as lavish as you'd expect a Carnegie heiress to have; she became known as "the Queen of Ohio" due to her extraordinary displays of wealth. Like a dog chasing its own tail, the money just reinforced the idea that Chadwick was already wealthy, which in turn made it possible for her to get even more money.

Her masterstroke was this idea that she was a "secret"—that is, illegitimate—daughter. Bank managers were too embarrassed to ask the Carnegie family if this scandalous information was true. And it wasn't just bank managers. Wealthy people in Cleveland were also willing to lend Chadwick money. Her problems began when one of her lenders wanted to be paid back. Chadwick refused, and this sparked a closer inspection of the many lies she'd told and documents she'd forged. Finally someone did contact Andrew Carnegie himself to ask about his mysterious lost daughter. He flatly declared he'd never heard of Cassie Chadwick. Chadwick was tried and convicted of conspiracy and sentenced to fourteen years in prison. She died just two years into her sentence.

A century later a fraudster named Christian Karl Gerhartsreiter lived the high life for two decades, from 1985 to 2006, pretending to be a member of the super-wealthy Rockefeller family. In this case, "Clark Rockefeller's" scheme was undone by his own wife, Sandra. She'd married him believing he was a Rockefeller but eventually became suspicious about the fact that he never seemed to have any money. Strangely enough, that's not the only case of a Rockefeller impersonator! A Frenchman named Christophe Rocancourt moved to Hollywood and convinced film producers that he was a member of the "French branch" of the Rockefeller family. The action star Jean-Claude Van Damme even produced a film for Rocancourt before the French faker was finally busted in 1998.

Another small-time impostor and con artist named David Hampton was immortalized in the play and subsequent film *Six Degrees of Separation*. One night in 1983, Hampton and a friend talked their way into the disco called Studio 54. They pretended to be celebrity relatives. Hampton said he was the son of actor Sidney Poitier, while his friend claimed to be the son of Gregory Peck. Their lie worked so well that Hampton decided to keep it up. First he posed as "David Poitier" simply to get free meals in restaurants, but soon he was convincing wealthy New Yorkers to let him stay over in their apartments. He would often rob them before disappearing. Some of his victims were celebrities themselves, such as fashion designer Calvin Klein. Ironically the play and film made Hampton legitimately famous, thereby totally ruining his con.

## What He Did for Love

Right now, in a high-security prison in Texas, there is a man serving a 144-year prison sentence. He spends twenty-three hours a day in solitary confinement. He is allowed no physical contact with other humans. Is he a serial killer? A terrorist? Nope. He is Steven Jay Russell, a world-class impostor with some fourteen aliases. These days Russell is held in maximum security because he managed to escape from four different jails within five years.

In 1992 Russell was sent to jail in Harris County, Texas, on minor fraud charges: he had faked a back injury for the insurance money. But there was a big problem. Russell's boyfriend, Jim Kemple, was suffering from AIDS at the time. Russell worried that Kemple would die by the time he got out of jail. The only option, in Russell's view, was to escape so he could join Kemple.

Russell stole some street clothes and a walkie-talkie. Then he changed out of his prison jumpsuit and simply strolled up to the prison gates.

Because of the police-issued walkie-talkie, prison guards assumed Russell was an undercover cop. They let him literally walk right out of prison. Russell and Kemple fled to Mexico, which is where this story probably should have ended. But it didn't.

## FAKERS ON FILM

Hollywood can't resist a crazy, true-life story, and Steven Russell's life was turned into the 2009 film *I Love You Phillip Morris*.[31] It wasn't the first time fakers of various stripes have been portrayed in film. A painfully incomplete list of the other greats includes:

*Trouble in Paradise* (1932): A pair of con artists team up to rob the owner of a perfume company and end up in a love triangle.

*The Lady Eve* (1941): Henry Fonda and Barbara Stanwyck star in this classic comedy about con artists who all target the same millionaire aboard a cruise ship.

*The Music Man* (1962): A con man gets more than he bargained for when he tangles with a small-town librarian.

*The Producers* (1967): Mel Brooks wrote and directed this classic comedy about a long con on Broadway. A film was also made of the musical version in 2005.

*Paper Moon* (1973): Real-life father and daughter Ryan and Tatum O'Neal play a con artist and a sassy orphan during the Great Depression.

*The Sting* (1973): In what is arguably *the* classic con-artist film, Paul Newman and Robert Redford run a type of long con that's sometimes called the Big Store.

*Dirty Rotten Scoundrels* (1988): A fun, silly movie starring Michael Caine and Steve Martin as rival con artists competing to steal from an American heiress.

*Leap of Faith* (1992): Another from Steve Martin: this time he's playing a con artist/televangelist. His character is based on Peter Popoff, whose story can be found on page 54.

*Catch Me If You Can* (2002): An exciting chase movie about an impostor named Frank Abagnale and the FBI agent determined to arrest him.

---

[31] This film is (justifiably) rated R; all the ones on the list that follows are PG-13 or lower.

Health and money problems eventually forced the two men to return to the United States, where Russell was quickly caught and sent back to prison. Unfortunately Kemple died soon after.

But in 1995 Russell found new love with an inmate named Phillip Morris. Morris was serving a short sentence for probation violation and "nonreturn" of a rental car.[30] Morris was released first, and Russell was paroled soon after. When the two were living together in Houston, Russell applied for a high-paying job as chief financial officer (CFO) with an insurance company. In truth the only experience Russell had with insurance was the fraud he'd been jailed for years earlier, but that didn't matter. He created a convincing fake resume, and he included numerous phone numbers for character references, all of which were actually Russell disguising his voice. Russell gave himself glowing reviews, and he was hired.

Yet again Russell had beaten the system. Yet again he had an opportunity to live out his life as a free man. And yet again he chose a different path.

As CFO he stole eight hundred thousand dollars from his company within five months. Russell claims the theft was motivated by his sense of justice. He wanted revenge for the cruel way he felt insurance companies had treated his late boyfriend, Jim Kemple. Others have suggested that the expensive tastes of his new boyfriend also had a bit to do with it—the couple owned multiple Mercedes-Benzes and matching Rolex watches.

Soon Russell was arrested on theft charges that brought a potential forty-five-year sentence. His bail was set at close to one million dollars, but Russell had other ideas. Calling the clerk's office from a prison phone, he impersonated his own judge and managed to get his bail reduced to forty-five thousand dollars. He paid it with what would turn out to be a fake check. And he was free again, but only briefly. Russell was arrested

---

[30] Aka *stealing* a rental car!

again, and he escaped again, this time by impersonating a doctor. He stole green Magic Markers one at a time from the prison art room. When he'd collected enough, he used the ink to dye his clothes green so that they looked like surgical scrubs. And in a pattern that was becoming embarrassingly familiar to Texas correctional officers, Steven Russell walked right out of prison.

But every time he escaped, he'd go straight back to Phillip Morris, which meant that Texas police never had to look very hard in order to find him. And so Russell was arrested yet again. This time, in 1998, he set in motion his most complex escape plan. The first thing he did was stop eating, to lose weight as quickly as possible. Then he used the interprison mail system to get fake medical records added to his file. The forged records claimed that Russell had AIDS. Amazingly, Texas authorities never tested Russell for the disease—they just took the forged documents at face value.

Between Russell's fake symptoms—which he knew well, having been through the disease with his first boyfriend—and the fake records, it was then a fairly simple matter to get himself transferred to a hospice program for the gravely ill. From there Russell impersonated his own doctor, called the hospice from an inside line, and got himself sent to a yet another treatment center for an experimental AIDS program. The thing was, no such center existed. In reality Russell went back to Phillip Morris. After some time passed, Russell called the hospice one final time, to have himself declared dead.

Alas, Texas authorities figured out that Russell was not dead at all, and he was arrested for what may be the final time. The man some call a modern Houdini is serving more than one hundred years for his escapes plus several additional decades for the embezzlement charges.

In 2010 he told a reporter he had no plans to try to escape again . . . but that he did wish Phillip Morris would come and visit.

## Catfishing

Every impostor is faced with a very basic challenge: How do you convince other people that you are who you say you are? Sometimes this is pretty easy. David Hampton just started introducing himself as David Poitier and doors immediately opened to him. Other times there's more trickery involved. Cassie Chadwick had to forge a lot of paperwork to pull off her "lost Carnegie" scam, just as Russell had to pretend to be many different people in many different phone calls. But what if being an impostor were much, much easier? What if you didn't even have to leave your house, much less change out of your pajamas? The Internet has changed a lot of things—not least the world of the impostor. If you can't see the people you're chatting with, you can't be 100 percent sure they are who they say they are. This has been great in some ways—for example, people can report on bad behaviors of companies or governments while keeping their identities secret. But it has also opened up a whole new arena for hoaxers to explore.

Sure, companies like Facebook try to force people to be honest about their online identities. But the reality is, there is very little on social media that can't be altered or faked, one way or another. And some people make a game out of pretending to be who they are not. The original term for an online pseudonym[32] was *sock puppet*. People use sock puppets to run up the scores in online polls. Other people use them to post outrageous opinions on websites.

In a 2010 documentary film, a young man who was carrying on a romance with a girl online found out that the girl didn't really exist. Someone online was pretending to be this invented woman. That film is called *Catfish*, and now that word gets used for all of these situations. Catfishing involves creating a fake identity online and then carrying on a relationship with someone who doesn't know that the identity isn't real. Sometimes people catfish because they are hoping to get money from their victims. Sometimes those who catfish already know their victims and are trying to hurt them. Sometimes people do it with no bad intent—they make up new identities just for fun. But it's not much fun if you're the person whose heart gets broken.

## The Sad Tale of Manti Te'o

A famous catfishing incident involved Manti Te'o, a football star from Hawaii. As a linebacker for the University of Notre Dame, Te'o was both massively talented and massively popular with fans. He led the team to an undefeated season in 2012 and was well on his way to becoming a superstar. A pair of tragedies added to his mystique: both his beloved grandmother and his girlfriend, named Lennay Kekua, had died within six hours of each other. Te'o told reporters that before she died, his girl-

---

[32] Pseudonyms are fake names that some authors use. Like how Mark Twain was the pseudonym of Samuel Clemens, or Lemony Snicket's real name is Daniel Handler, or H.P. Wood's real name is ????

friend had made him promise that he would play in the "big game" against Michigan rather than attend her funeral. The tragic tale of Te'o and Kekua's doomed romance became inseparable from Te'o's status as a football star.

But in January 2013, a sports website called Deadspin published a bombshell: there was no Lennay Kekua. The whole thing was a hoax.

Suspicion fell on another football player, Ronaiah Tuiasosopo. In time he admitted that he'd posed as Kekua, both online and by phone. He used photos of a pretty girl he knew on Facebook and claimed those were pictures of Kekua. Tuiasosopo told TV host Dr. Phil that he perpetrated the hoax because he had feelings for Te'o but was trying to "recover" from being gay.

The big question, which might never be perfectly answered, is what Te'o knew and when he knew it. Some accused Te'o of knowing he'd been catfished but deliberately lying about his

*Notre Dame linebacker Manti Te'o. A victim of fraud? Or a fraudster himself?*

dead girlfriend as a publicity stunt anyway. But the more likely explanation is probably the simplest: Te'o was catfished. His uncle told a reporter, "Our kids are raised to be obedient. They're not raised to be skeptical." As for Te'o, he still says that "the relationship, to me, was real."

# CHAPTER 6

## I Want to Believe: Science Hoaxes

Scientists use techniques like observation, measurement, and experimentation to try to better understand the world we live in. The whole point of the scientific method is to rely on techniques like measurement and observation, and not allow preconceived ideas to influence discoveries. But as much as they try, scientists are still human beings. Consequently, they can both hoax others and be hoaxed themselves.

### The Rabbit Woman

The year is 1726. There are no cars, televisions, or cell phones. It was a time before pretty much all your favorite stuff was invented.

Imagine that you live in England, in a small village called Godalming. You're a young woman with three kids. You work outside in the fields all day, every day. When it rains, when it snows, even when you're pregnant—you plant crops, pull weeds, and dig holes. It's tiring, dirty, boring work. But that's your life, and there's no reason for you to suspect it will ever change.

Maybe you'd like to see London, the capital city, just one time in your life. But London is almost forty miles away. In the twenty-first century, the trip between London and Godalming will take about an hour. But in your current time, in 1726? For an illiterate peasant, London may as well be in Australia.[33]

So, that's your situation. What would you do?

Mary Toft was just this kind of young woman. In her quest to get out of Godalming, she made herself into one of the biggest celebrities of eighteenth-century England. How? She convinced some of the most educated men in the country that she was the mother of an entire warren of rabbits.

The hoax began in September 1726, when Mary convinced a local doctor named John Howard that she had just given birth to some sort of monster that was part cat, part eel, and part rabbit. But then she settled on birthing rabbits only. Under Howard's care, she produced more than a dozen dead rabbits (or pieces of rabbits) over the next few days. Howard began a letter-writing campaign to try to gain the attention of experts around Britain.

He was successful. Mary soon became a celebrity, and many doctors wanted to examine her. Even King George sent members of his private medical team to investigate the Rabbit Woman of Godalming. Some doctors believed her and some didn't, but they all wanted to see this supposed miracle for themselves. Meanwhile Mary Toft sent her husband out to buy more baby rabbits in secret. She inserted them, the doctors removed them, and the hoax continued on this way for weeks.

To understand how this could happen, it's important to realize that medicine was in a strange phase in this era. Female midwives, who had been in charge of delivering babies for a very long time, were being pushed out of business by male doctors. The widely respected Dr. John Maubray expressed a common opinion when he said that men were "better versed in anatomy, better acquainted with [surgical techniques], and [possessed] greater presence of mind" than women. Ironically the large egos of many

---

[33] Which, by the way, has not been invented at this point, either.

of these doctors made them even more vulnerable to Mary's hoax. The idea that a young woman might have fooled them was *impossible* for many of them to believe.

It's also important to understand that in the eighteenth century, it was considered inappropriate for male doctors to look too closely at the private areas of their female patients. Some doctors even covered their patients with a sheet so they could deliver babies without actually *seeing* the women's bodies. It's fair to say that in 1726, the average doctor's understanding of female anatomy was shaky at best.

Mary Toft also took advantage of a myth that was widely believed at the time: "maternal impression." The idea was that if a pregnant woman either dreamed about an animal or was startled by one, her baby would have some of the characteristics of that animal. Mary claimed that she chased a rabbit one day while she was pregnant, and that she spent the next few nights dreaming of rabbits at night and longing to eat them during the day. Hard to believe, but this actually seemed reasonable to people at the time.

Another widely accepted bit of nonsense was the belief in black, mole-like creatures called sooterkins. Supposedly if a pregnant woman stood too close to a stove, she would give birth to a sooterkin instead of a baby. One advocate of sooterkins was none other than Dr. John Maubray, one of Mary Toft's biggest defenders.

The Rabbit Woman hoax was eventually undone by simple geography. The king's doctors insisted that she be brought to London for further study. Once there Mary could no longer get any rabbits. After time passed with no more bunnies appearing, suspicions began to grow.

A famous doctor named Sir Richard Manningham was a Rabbit Woman skeptic. He got Mary Toft to confess by threatening to operate on her unless she told the truth. Rather than submit to being cut open, she admitted the hoax. Toft was jailed briefly, but officials soon realized they weren't sure *precisely* what laws she had broken. Plus, her presence in London was an embarrassment to the powerful members of the Court who had been fooled by her. So Toft was quietly released from jail and allowed to leave. (Where she went after this is not totally clear, but she was arrested one other time for selling stolen goods.) The Rabbit Woman scandal ruined the careers of a number of doctors, many of whom spent years defending themselves from accusations of being gullible idiots.

In her confession, Mary Toft also explained *why* she began the hoax. She told Manningham of her hope that, if she became famous, she'd get a regular allowance from the king and no longer have to work in the fields.

If you think about Mary Toft's life, can you blame her? And although she never got that allowance, she did at least get out of Godalming.

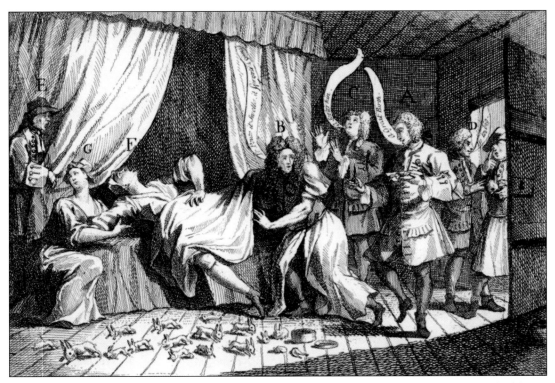

*William Hogarth illustration—"The Cunicularii," a pun on* cuniculus, *which is Latin for a type of rabbit— mocks the many so-called experts who were fooled by Mary Toft. The letters on the illustration were used to identify particular suckers by name—they would have all been infamous at the time the illustration was created.*

## The Lying Stones

The year 1726 was an oddly bad one for scientific truth. At the same time Toft's hoax was playing out in England, a different one was underway over in Germany. While out on a walk, a respected scientist named Johan Beringer discovered a treasure trove of amazing limestone "fossils." These stones had images of things like slugs and frogs, birds in flight, spiders in webs, and even stars in the sky. Some of the stones were inscribed with the name "Jehovah" (God)—some in Hebrew, some in Babylonian, and some in Arabic.

And so now we get to learn a wonderful German word: *Lügensteine*, for lying stones.

Beringer, a professor at the University of Würzburg, was convinced the stones were real fossils. Other experts pointed out that the images appeared to have been carved by hand. But to Beringer, that didn't matter. He published an entire book about the stones: *Lithographiae Wirceburgensis*. One chapter in his book was devoted to the question of whether the stones were a hoax. Beringer concluded that the fact that the stones *appeared* fake was just God testing human faith.

It turns out, though, that the stones were actually carved by two of Beringer's colleagues: J. Ignatz Roderick and Georg von Eckhart. Amazingly, Roderick and Eckhart even tried to confess their fraud to Beringer, but he accused *them* of being the liars, not the stones! Much like the doctors who invested too much in Mary Toft's story, Beringer had staked his career and reputation on these stones. He could no longer see reason.

It wasn't until Beringer found a "fossil" that was carved with his *own* name that he accepted the truth. He felt so ashamed that he spent all his money buying up copies of his own book to try to make the whole thing disappear. He also sued Roderick and Eckhart. During the court case, the hoaxers explained that they made the stones to embarrass Beringer, who was widely disliked by other professors at the university.

## The Piltdown Man

You probably noticed that the cases of the Rabbit Woman and the Lying Stones both involved scientists being outfoxed by others. On the other hand, the Fujimura case (see box) was an example of a scientist faking his own discovery. Unfortunately Fujimura was far from the first one to try this.

For instance, ever since Charles Darwin published *On the Origin of Species* (1859), archaeologists had been on the hunt for fossils that would clarify the process of human evolution. Back then, most people envisioned an unbroken chain—a straight line that began with apes and ended with humans. (We now understand that evolution is more complex than this.) But at the time, what really bugged scientists was an obvious blank spot in the chain. They called it "the missing link."

Then in 1912, Charles Dawson—not Darwin!—convinced experts

## THE DEVIL'S DIVINE HANDS

In 1981 Shinichi Fujimura claimed to have discovered stoneware from the Paleolithic period outside Tokyo. This was an amazing find, because archaeologists had never thought that human settlements in Japan dated back that far.

The discovery was even more remarkable because Fujimura was an amateur. He worked for a manufacturing company but spent much of his time with a hobbyist archaeology group called Sekki Bunka Kenkyukai. The group was responsible for a number of important finds in the late 1970s and 1980s. Fujimura was particularly known for his ability to locate artifacts completely on his own. People said he had "divine hands."

It turned out that Fujimura was using his "divine hands" to plant the discoveries himself. In 2000 a newspaper hid a camera near one of his sites. Fujimura was caught digging holes in order to create his archaeological discoveries. Confronted with this evidence, he confessed. The Japanese Archaeological Association investigated Fujimura's work and concluded that nearly everything he'd ever found was faked. When asked why, Fujimura said tearfully, "The devil made me do it."

around the world that he had found an ancient skull that could fill in that space. An amateur archaeologist, Dawson found the skull near an English village called Piltdown, so his discovery came to be known as the Piltdown Man. Dawson's work was aided by no less than Arthur Smith Woodward, who was the keeper of geology at Britain's Natural History Museum. He and Dawson reconstructed the skull together. Meanwhile further digging at the Piltdown site turned up a jawbone, teeth, and primitive tools.

According to *Scientific American*, the discovery of the Piltdown Man scratched a very particular itch among scientists. They agreed that humans had evolved from apes, but the skulls that had been found up to that point looked extremely ape-like, with smallish brains and "snout-like" faces. It wasn't a good look. Scientists were eager for the discovery of an ancient skull that reminded them of themselves. With its narrow forehead and large brain capacity, the Piltdown Man was much more to scientists' liking. Even better: it was British! Didn't that suggest that humankind originated in Great Britain? To English scientists, the Piltdown Man was like a dream come true.

The Piltdown Man was accepted as real for more than thirty years. But in the late 1940s, new tests were invented to determine the age of artifacts. When those tests were performed on the Piltdown Man, scientists discovered that the skull was about only fifty thousand years old. That's really old, but not *nearly* old enough to qualify as a "missing link."

But, hey, it happens. Everybody makes mistakes, right? Well . . .

As it turned out, this had been more than an accident. Investigators finally realized that the skull had been dyed to match the gravel in Piltdown. The jawbone was probably from an orangutan, with its teeth filed to appear like human teeth. The Piltdown Man was no innocent mistake: it was a cleverly crafted, deliberate fake.

The evidence was finally made public in 1953. Newspaper headlines shouted, "Fossil Hoax Makes Monkeys Out of Scientists."

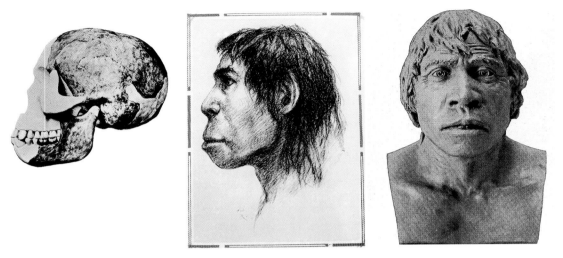

*Here are three renditions of the fake Piltdown man: the skull itself, an illustration of what he supposedly looked like, and a clay version of our nonexistent ancestor.*

The question remains: Was Charles Dawson responsible for the hoax, or was he fooled by someone else? We'll never know for sure. Over the years, a number of other people have been suggested as possible coconspirators. One is of course Arthur Smith Woodward, the man who helped Dawson with the initial discovery. Another suspect is Martin Hinton, a disgruntled employee of the Natural History Museum. A third, believe it or not, is Sir Arthur Conan Doyle, creator of the fictional detective Sherlock Holmes. Doyle belonged to the same amateur archaeology club as Dawson; he, Woodward, and Dawson all knew one another. Some people say that Doyle left hints about the Piltdown Man in his book *The Lost World* (1912).[34]

It's worth noting that when archaeologists examined Dawson's *private* collection, they found that more than a dozen of those were also fakes. And some were eerily similar to the Piltdown Man.

---

[34] *The Lost World* tells the story of a reporter and archaeologists traveling to a place in South America where dinosaurs still exist. Published the same year the Piltdown Man was found, it has a reference to the idea that bones are easy to fake. Some have taken that as a wink from Doyle that he helped Dawson, or at least knew about the hoax.

## The Tasaday Tribe

Until the Piltdown Man was revealed as a hoax, scientists were delighted to be in possession of this remnant of early human life. Imagine the excitement when *actual*, live "cavemen" were discovered.

In 1971 the Philippine government announced exactly that. A tribe of people called the Tasaday had been discovered, deep in the rain forest on the island of Mindanao. They were still living in caves, just as our prehistoric ancestors had done. They had no technology to speak of, and they dressed in clothing made from leaves. The Tasaday were a completely peaceful people—their language had no words for "war," "enemy," or anything violent. They didn't farm or hunt. Instead they survived solely on foods they could forage in the jungle, like berries and tadpoles.

The self-appointed protector of the Tasaday was Manuel Elizalde, a Harvard-educated employee of the Philippine government. Anthropologists, linguists, and journalists all longed to visit the Tasaday. The existence of a pure Stone Age culture, unaffected by the modern world, was a discovery of incalculable scientific value. But Elizalde used the Philippine army to keep strict control over who was allowed to visit the caves and who was not. And after some scientists wondered how the Tasaday could possibly live on berries and tadpoles—which, they noted, could supply only about a third of the caloric requirements of an average human—Elizalde decided it was better to keep the scientists out entirely.

He did permit a number of flattering media portrayals, including a highly influential *National Geographic* article, a documentary that aired on US television repeatedly, and a book called *The Gentle Tasaday* (1975). The story captured the imaginations of people all over the world.[35]

In 1983 Elizalde fled the country for reasons unrelated to the Tasaday.

---

[35] This includes a young girl in the United States who devoted her entire fourth-grade project to a study of the Tasaday and became very bitter when the hoax was revealed. But enough about me.

He took millions of dollars with him and hid out in Costa Rica before being expelled from that country as well. In the meantime, the corrupt Philippine government was overthrown in 1986. In all the confusion, journalists were again able to get access to the Tasaday tribe. They found that the caves were empty but the Tasaday were nearby, living in regular homes and wearing regular clothes. Tribe members said they had been paid by Elizalde to pretend to live in the caves, eat tadpoles, and so on. They said the whole thing was faked to fool anthropologists. Manuel Elizalde died in 1997, confessing nothing.

But the story takes an interesting turn from here. Some of the Tasaday claimed that their "confession" was misinterpreted—quite literally *misinterpreted*, as the Tasaday speak their own, distinct language. Linguists who have studied the Tasaday language argue that its uniqueness is evidence that the Tasaday people had, in fact, been living completely apart from modernity. The grass-wearing, tadpole-eating aspects of the Tasaday may have been fake, but the tribe is, indeed, distinct from all other people

*Members of the Tasaday tribe out of costume—this is how they actually dressed.*

in the Philippines. If this is true, Elizalde's crime is not that he invented lies about the Tasaday, but rather that he prevented the rest of us from learning what was *truly* special about this unique tribe.

## The Monkey Man

While it's true science hoaxes can include the medical, the archaeological, and the anthropological, another scientific field that has been prime for hoaxers over the years is astronomy. What many scientists want most is concrete *proof* of life beyond the stars. Over the years, hoaxers have been more than willing to provide it.

On July 8, 1953, a young Georgia man named Ed Watters made a discovery that threatened to overturn everything we think we know about the universe. He and two friends were driving in his pickup truck late at night when they came upon a glowing red spacecraft parked in the middle of the road. Three creatures, just a few feet tall, stood in front of the craft. Watters slammed on his brakes, but he wasn't quick enough to avoid hitting one of them. The other two aliens jumped into their spaceship and took off.

Later, a policeman found the young men, standing by Watters's truck in a state of shock. There was a large scorch mark on the road where the ship had taken off in a hurry. And there was one very dead alien. It was only about two feet tall at most, with long skinny legs and long skinny arms to match.

Unsure of what to do in this situation, the police officer allowed Watters and his friends to take the alien corpse home. They kept it overnight in their refrigerator, like you do.

The next day, the young men called the *Atlanta Journal-Constitution* about their amazing discovery. The newspaper engaged a local veterinarian to study the corpse, and the vet agreed that it was "something out of this world." The story went out all over the country, and various newspapers reported that a dead alien had been found.

The report also reached the Georgia State Police, who sent in their own experts to investigate. But it took anatomy professors Dr. Marlon Hines and Dr. W. A. Mickle of Emory University only a matter of minutes to realize that the "alien" was actually a shaved monkey whose tail had been removed. If the creature came from Mars, Dr. Hines said, "they have monkeys on Mars."

Confronted with this, Watters confessed. His friends had bet him ten dollars that he couldn't get his name in the paper within a week. So Watters bought a monkey (some sources say a capuchin monkey; some say rhesus), killed it, and altered the body to make it look more alien. The scorch marks in the road were faked with a blowtorch.

The bet was won, but between the money spent on the monkey and the fine paid for the hoax, Watters ended up feeling like he'd lost. He eventually moved out of Georgia entirely because he was so tired of people calling him "Monkey Man."

## Alien Autopsy

Until he got found out, Ed "Monkey Man" Watters was probably quite pleased to have gotten his name in a few newspapers. But Watters was an amateur compared to Ray Santilli. Santilli's UFO-related hoax is famous all over the world.

As every ufologist[36] knows, in July 1947 an alien ship supposedly crashed in the desert outside of Roswell, New Mexico. Now, whether the crash really involved an alien craft, a weather balloon, or a device for monitoring Soviet nuclear tests is a question we'll leave for another book. The point is, whatever evidence existed regarding the crash was top secret, which left very little for ufologists to go on.

To the rescue came a British music promoter named Ray Santilli. In the early 1990s, while looking for footage of Elvis, Santilli met a camera-

---

[36] Yes, that is so a word! A ufologist ("yoo-FOLL-uh-jist") is a person who studies unidentified flying objects.

man who had been serving in the US military at the time of the Roswell incident. The cameraman claimed that he had filmed the autopsies of the alien beings. The footage was, of course, top secret. But the cameraman, at this point retired and living in Clearwater, Florida, had kept a copy for himself. He had twenty-two reels of film, each reel lasting between four and five minutes. He offered to sell those reels to Santilli.

After a few years of negotiation and fund-raising, Santilli and a friend named Gary Shoefield bought the films. They screened the material publicly for the first time in 1995 at the Museum of London. About a hundred people were invited, including both ufologists and skeptics, as well as journalists and representatives of various religions. That audience was the first to see what would become world famous as the "Alien Autopsy." It is a grainy, black-and-white film with shaky camerawork that appears to show two army doctors performing an autopsy of one of the aliens while a third doctor takes notes. The doctors cut off the top of the alien's head to expose the brain; they take samples of its eyes; they open up its belly and take the organs out.

It's creepy. It's gruesome. It's fake.

The film aired in the United States as part of a TV special in 1995, and "Alien Autopsy" became a media sensation. But even then, there were

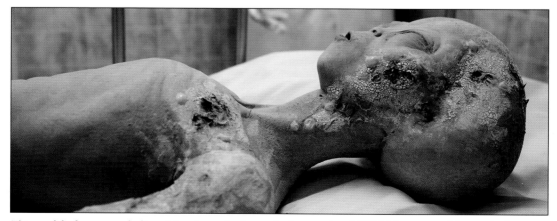

*This model of a supposed alien visitor is on display at the International UFO Museum and Research Center in New Mexico.*

doubters. Indeed, the director of the TV special expressed his skepticism *as he was making the show*. He was told by the network to keep those worries to himself. Other people pointed out various problems with the film: the alien looked rubbery and fake, the "doctors" didn't hold their scalpels like real doctors, and so on. Still, the majority of people who saw the footage found it compelling and believable.

Much of the curiosity surrounding the film centered on the mysterious cameraman. Who was he? Where was he? Santilli refused to say. He did release an interview with the man, in which his face is obscured by shadow. In the interview the cameraman confirms every detail of Santilli's story.

Finally in 2006 a British TV show called *Eamonn Investigates* aired lengthy interviews with Santilli and Shoefield. This time the men admitted that they had created the footage themselves. Host Eamonn Holmes even got Santilli and Shoefield to take him to the London home where the autopsy was filmed. A special-effects expert named John Humphreys also appeared on the show and explained how he made the alien. He'd made several aliens, actually, because the autopsy had to be performed

## NOT A FAKER!

As you read about all these science fakes, you can be forgiven for wondering whether there are as many scientists making things up as there are scientists finding things out! You wouldn't be the first to speculate on this question. It's a source of frustration for many scientists that goofy fakes like the ones in this chapter are met with wide-eyed belief, while some legitimate discoveries have to fight their way through many layers of doubt before being accepted.

For example, it took a very long time for scientists to be persuaded that the platypus is a real animal and not a hoax. The first scientific description of a platypus was written by George Shaw in 1799, but even after examining a platypus in person, Shaw wrote, "I almost doubt the testimony of my own eyes with respect to the structure of this animal's beak." Keep in mind, this was an era where people displayed their stuffed mermaids with total sincerity. So you really can't blame Shaw for wondering.

more than once. Humphreys used sheep brains, fruit jelly, and chicken guts to create the alien's gooey insides.

So Santilli and Shoefield finally fessed up. Right? Maybe, maybe not.

They told Holmes that the "Alien Autopsy" film was actually a "restoration" of an original film that Santilli swears he saw. Supposedly by the time Santilli bought the footage, the film had begun to degrade and was no longer watchable. So Santilli and Shoefield decided to *re-create* the autopsy and combine it with the tiny bits of the original that were still useable. Santilli admitted that "less than 5 percent" of the footage was from the original autopsy film, and he was reluctant to provide much detail about which 5 percent that would be.

There's something logic-defying about all this. Santilli and Shoefield never explained *why* they allowed people to believe the film was real for over ten years. Even rapidly degrading footage of an alien would have been a big story. Why not have the film restored by professionals? Similarly the "cameraman" Santilli interviewed was actually a homeless man from Los Angeles. Santilli found him on the street, took him to a hotel room, and told him what to say to the camera. Santilli claimed he did this to "throw [people] off the trail" of the real cameraman. Why this was necessary or how it would work isn't clear. The cameraman had never been found—there was no "trail." There was only Santilli's claim that the man existed at all.

So was there ever an alien-autopsy film? And if so, did Santilli really see it? Or is this new cover story just an extension of the original hoax? You can make up your own mind. I'll give you my view, though: The Alien Autopsy is, to adapt a famous statement by Winston Churchill, a prank wrapped in a hoax inside a fraud. There are legitimate scientists who are searching for alien life—for instance, the SETI (Search for Extraterrestrial Intelligence) Institute in Mountain View, California. None of their work involves watching poorly lit videos of gooey gray men.

# CHAPTER 7

## Snake Oil: Deception in Medicine

In the seventeenth and eighteenth centuries, medicine was a mysterious and unreliable field. That's a polite way of saying the majority of well-intentioned doctors didn't know what they were doing.[37] Ignorance made medicine a prime arena for fakers and swindlers.

Two hundred years ago, the European continent was swarming with men known as mountebanks. Mountebanks were a blend of traveling salesman and carnival act. They stood on makeshift wooden platforms and made entertaining speeches about whatever miracle cure they happened to be selling that day. Some mountebanks were amateur dentists, and they'd offer to pull out people's rotten teeth right there on the platform. Usually there was also a clown involved; in Italy, the performers were called *zanni*, which is where our English word *zany* comes from.

Mountebanks traveled throughout Europe, but they must have been particularly common in the Netherlands, because numerous Dutch painters used mountebanks as their subjects. In the Netherlands, these showmen were not called mountebanks but *kwakzalver*. At the time,

---

[37] Check out the story of the Rabbit Woman in chapter 6 to recall how clueless even "good" doctors could be.

*kwaken* was Dutch for bragging or boasting, and *zalver* meant seller of salve.[38] The world's first "skeptic" organization was founded in the Netherlands in 1881, and it was called Vereniging tegen de Kwakzalverij, or the Society Against Quackery. It's from Old Dutch that we get our modern expression *quacks*—bad doctors.

As far as America goes, once the colonies were founded, the mountebanks weren't far behind. In 1757 a historian named William Smith wrote that in the New York colony, "Quacks abound like Locusts in Egypt." In typical American style, the small-time performances common in Europe got bigger and fancier as time went on. It wasn't enough to have one mountebank and a clown—no, sir. American pitchmen would add a singer, an acrobat, and maybe some magic tricks.

Soon these full-scale medicine shows were as elaborate—and as popular—as any traveling circus. The pitch doctors, as they were known, had theatrical names like the Diamond King, Dr. Painless Parker, and Silk Hat Harry. Their product names were just as creative: Hamlin's Wizard Oil . . . Cholera Balm . . . Kickapoo Joy Juice. At the height of their popularity in the 1890s, traveling medicine shows would last around two hours and include dancers, animal acts, and displays of sharpshooting. It was all done in the name of whatever product the pitchman was selling. Most often the shows sold ointments and syrups, but other so-called cures were offered as well. A number of pitchmen claimed they could heal people with magnets. One pitchman, appropriately named Dr. Mud, traveled around southeast Texas selling special dirt-based treatments.

There were plenty of small-time con men involved in traveling medicine shows, and they'd sell bottles of whatever homemade nonsense they could cook up in a bathtub the night before. But some of the businesses got quite large and complicated. The Kickapoo Medicine Company, for example, claimed to produce Native American–made treatments. Their

---

[38] A salve is a healing ointment, as in the expression "salve your wounds."

*A mountebank sells his wares in* The Quack, *painted by Jan Steen sometime between 1650 and 1660.*

products, however, were actually shipped out of a massive warehouse in New Haven, Connecticut.

Like most fads, the medicine show faded away in time, a victim of changing public tastes. Thanks to radio, movies, and television, people found other ways to pass the time. That's not to say that people lost interest in miracle cures. No, only the sales channels changed. Cheap, widely available newspapers meant that as interest in medicine shows faded, a new genre of hokum expanded: patent medicines.

The name *patent medicine* is itself kind of a con. After all, a patent is an official government recognition that there is something new and useful about an invention. There was very little new or useful in most patent medicines, and most patent medicines were not patented. Sold mainly by means of newspaper advertisements, patent medicines were concoctions that claimed to cure literally anything that ailed a person, from a bad cough to cancer and everything in between. A lot of these medicines contained what we now consider serious drugs, including alcohol, heroin, and cocaine. No doubt they made people feel better for a while, but they sure didn't cure you of anything.

## Selling Snake Oil

You've probably heard the expression *snake-oil salesman*, in reference to a certain type of person—a crooked politician, for example—who makes a lot of empty promises. The expression comes to us from the medicine shows of the Wild West.

In the nineteenth century, immigrants from China came to the west coast of the United States in growing numbers, and they brought their traditional medicine with them. Chinese healers were well aware of the healing properties of certain kinds of snakes. Laborers used to rub salves made from Chinese water snakes and mud snakes on aching muscles. And, indeed, modern science confirms that those types of snakes do contain substances, including omega-3s and certain acids, that could make them legitimately useful.

Of course, there weren't any Chinese water snakes in the American West. What the region did have, in spades, was rattlesnakes. So pitch doctors used them instead. Unlike the Chinese snakes, rattlesnakes have little or no healing qualities—not that this mattered to the medicine shows.

The most famous snake-oil salesman was Clark Stanley, who sold his Snake Oil Liniment all over the West and even made a splash at the World's Fair in Chicago in 1893. Stanley made a big feature of killing and boiling rattlesnakes live on stage. He claimed that the fat that rose to the top was the secret ingredient in his powerful medicine.

Years later, Stanley's Snake Oil Liniment was analyzed in a lab. The result? Not only was his product nothing like the Chinese original, there was no snake in the Snake Oil *at all*. Those rattlesnakes Stanley killed were just part of the show. His liniment was made from mineral oil, beef fat, and red pepper, with a little turpentine added to make it smell like medicine.

## Patent Killer: The Story of Arthur Cramp

The best that patent medicines could do was not much. The worst they could do was make sickness worse or even kill. In 1906 the US Congress

### THE WORST ROCKEFELLER

The Rockefeller family got rich in the early 1900s thanks to their company, Standard Oil. But they could never completely hide the fact that their dynasty had its roots in oil of a different sort: snake oil.

William Avery Rockefeller was born in 1810. He traveled around selling trinkets while pretending to be both deaf and mute in order to gain sympathy. Handsome and charming, Rockefeller had a number of relationships: one with a poor woman named Nancy Brown and another with a wealthy woman named Eliza Davidson. William married Eliza, but kept Nancy around as their housekeeper and had children by both women. It was Eliza's kids, John and William Jr., who later founded Standard Oil.

Their father never stayed home for long—he was usually off selling "botanical elixirs" under the name William Levingston, Herbal Doctor. He eventually abandoned his family completely.

When John Rockefeller became the world's first billionaire, newspapers tried to ferret out his "dark family secret." Newspaper editor Joseph Pulitzer offered a reward to anyone who could prove that the rumors about "Doc Rockefeller" were true. But the story of the snake-oil salesman stayed hidden for many years.

William Rockefeller died in 1906 without ever being acknowledged as the billionaire's father. Which is OK, because William Rockefeller was the worst.

passed the Pure Food and Drug Act, an effort to try and stop unscrupu-
lous companies from selling tainted food and ineffective medicine. The
American Medical Association (AMA) also got involved, devoting an
entire wing of its organization to exposing fraud and false claims about
medicines.

This effort was led by a man with a quiet voice but a very loud pen.
Dr. Arthur J. Cramp was a British immigrant who came to the United
States in 1892. He was an English teacher in Wisconsin when his only
daughter died after being treated by a quack doctor. Heartbroken and
outraged, Cramp resolved that he would not sit by and let quacks continue to hurt more patients. He enrolled in medical school and took a
job with the AMA as soon as he graduated. Cramp devoted his life to
exposing medical fraud in all its forms.

One of his most significant achievements was the massive book *Nostrums and Quackery*. Originally published in 1911 at five hundred pages,
the book exposed every bit of evidence Cramp could find about all kinds
of medical scams. *Nostrums and Quackery* quickly sold out and was
reprinted in a second edition, this time at seven hundred pages. Then in
1921 Cramp released yet another volume of entirely new scams, this one
running eight hundred pages.

Cramp described *Nostrums and Quackery* as "a veritable 'Who's Who
in Quackdom.'" And he didn't hold back. In the chapter called "Baby
Killers," Cramp lists names and ages of young American children who
were poisoned by patent medicines like Kopp's Baby Friend and Mrs.
Winslow's Soothing Syrup.

The problem, of course, was that no sooner did Cramp expose one
fraud than another sprang up in its place. These days, quacks don't place
ads in newspapers anymore; online is where the action is. Today's tricks
include anti-aging miracles, marvelous memory boosters, magical weight-
loss pills, and dangerous fake cures for real illnesses like arthritis, cancer,

and AIDS. If it sounds too good to be true, keep in mind the lessons of Dr. Arthur Cramp: it probably is.

## The Curing Powers of Electricity?

The main focus of Cramp's work was patent medicines, but his investigations didn't stop there. In fact, Cramp's primary nemesis didn't sell medicines at all. His name was Dr. Albert Abrams, and Cramp declared him to be "the dean of twentieth-century charlatans."

For the first half of his life, Abrams was quite well respected. At an impressively young age, he earned a medical degree from the prestigious University of Heidelberg in Germany. Then around midlife, Abrams's life took a very different path.

First he began publishing about his belief that all illnesses had a direct connection to the spine. This delighted practitioners of the young field called "chiropractic," which had been founded in 1895 by D. D. Palmer. But Abrams didn't stop there. Soon he was claiming that every illness had a unique electrical signature. Abrams declared that he could diagnose patients based on one drop of blood by means of his invention, the dynamizer.

Actually the invention was more complex than that. It involved four separate but interconnected machines. First there was the dynamizer, where the blood went. Then there was something called a rheostatic dynamizer, which was connected to the first machine with a wire. Connected to that was the vibratory rate rheostat, and finally the measuring rheostat. Here's the really weird part—a healthy person (that is, someone other than the patient!) would be hooked up to the measuring rheostat. Abrams called that person the *reagent*. By tapping on the reagent's torso, Abrams claimed to be able to identify the electrical impulses that were causing the illness in the original patient's blood sample. And—this is important!—the reagent had to be facing west for the dynamizer to work correctly. Otherwise, forget it.

The entire contraption was called ERA, for Electronic Reactions of Abrams. It was, in the words of scientist Robert Millikan, the kind of device "a ten-year-old would build to fool an eight-year-old." Abrams insisted that the ERA could detect all manner of illnesses, even using the blood samples of dead people. He diagnosed the long-deceased writers Samuel Pepys, Henry Wadsworth Longfellow, and Edgar Allan Poe with the disease called syphilis.

And, as the advertisements say, *How much would you pay for an ERA device? But wait, there's more!* In 1922 Abrams published an article claiming he could also use his ERA device to guess a patient's religion.

He went on to invent a different machine, called an oscilloclast, which was a box with electrodes attached. Abrams claimed that by hooking a patient up to the box, the oscilloclast could neutralize the electrical impulses that were causing the person's problem. Yes, you heard right: first Abrams invented a gadget to diagnose a problem, then he invented a second gadget to cure whatever problem the first gadget had identified.

## SYNDROME K

In autumn 1943 parts of Italy were under German occupation. The Nazis began rounding up Italian Jews and sending them to concentration camps. But when they arrived at Fatebenefratelli Hospital in Rome, they learned about an outbreak of a ghastly disease called Syndrome K. This Syndrome K was wildly infectious, and anyone who contracted it would die quickly and painfully. The doctors argued that the patients should remain quarantined in the hospital, rather than sent to camps where they could expose soldiers and guards to their terrible illness. And when the Nazis heard the desperate cries and hacking coughs coming from the wards, they quickly agreed. Decades later, one of the doctors, Vittorio Sacerdoti, told a reporter that the Nazis "fled like rabbits."

But here's the thing: there's no such disease. A diagnosis of Syndrome K was simply code for "this person must be hidden from the Nazis." The doctors had managed to make the Germans terrified of a completely imaginary condition, even coaching patients to cough and moan on cue. Several dozen innocent lives were spared by this heroic bit of medical fakery.

Abrams sold ERA devices to the general public, but would only rent the oscilloclast—at a high fee, of course.

If all this sounds fishy to you, good! But many people were fooled, and Abrams became a very rich man.

Here's where the irony gets really thick: Dr. Cramp and the AMA hired the journalist Upton Sinclair to write an exposé of Abrams in 1922. Sinclair was a famous "muckraker" whose book *The Jungle* had helped inspire the passage of the Pure Food and Drug Act. Instead of exposing the hoax, Sinclair was completely taken in by it. Rather than a *Jungle*-style takedown, Sinclair wrote a starry-eyed ode to Abrams called "The House of Wonder." According to Sinclair, in Abrams's office "the blind begin to see, the deaf begin to hear, the lame begin to walk!"

Fortunately everyone did not fall for these wild claims about the powers of the ERA. For example, one skeptic sent Abrams a vial of blood for diagnosis, and Abrams responded that he had found signs of not only cancer, but also the grim-sounding condition genitourinary tuberculosis. But the *really* important detail that the dynamizer failed to detect was that the blood sample came from a chicken.

Since the Sinclair exposé was an embarrassing failure, the magazine *Scientific American* began its own long-term investigation of Albert Abrams. Many hoped that the series of articles would result in Abrams's arrest or, at the very least, admission of guilt. Alas, in January 1924, before the complete series of articles could be published, Abrams died of pneumonia.[39] He left behind an estate of well over two million dollars, and his heirs spent the next few years in court fighting over it.

## Diet Through Chocolate

Dr. Arthur Cramp is no longer with us, but fortunately there are still lots of skeptics doing the hard work of exposing today's medical fakes. To take

---

[39] Apparently there was at least *one* illness the oscilloclast couldn't cure!

just one example, in late 2014, some German TV producers were working on a documentary about fake diet products. They approached a science writer named John Bohannon to help them with an experiment. Bohannon had already done some work with the magazine *Science* to expose unethical journals that published bad studies for a fee.

Bohannon and a German doctor named Dr. Gunter Frank conducted a research project designed to prove that "scientific studies" are not always very scientific. They created a real clinical trial, just like the kind used by doctors all the time—but their trial was to prove the absurd claim that chocolate was a health food. A third of the participants went on a low carbohydrate diet; another third went on the same diet but also ate a bar of dark chocolate every day; and the final third, the control group, ate normally. Bohannon and Frank weren't completely sure what they were going to discover, so they measured a large range of things, including weight loss, cholesterol levels, sodium levels, and so on.

After three weeks the participants were weighed and measured, and the results were shocking: the group that ate chocolate lost weight 10 percent faster than the other groups. They also had better cholesterol levels. Alert the media!

Bohannon and Frank reported their findings using a fake but impressive-sounding name: the Institute of Diet and Health. Predictably the online media grabbed the chocolate story and ran with it. Headlines blared "Excellent News: Chocolate Can Help You Lose Weight!" and "Why You Must Eat Chocolate Daily." The chocolate weight-loss story appeared in magazines and on websites all over the world.

Here's the kicker: the study had only fifteen participants. As Bohannon wrote later, "Here's a dirty little science secret: if you measure a large number of things about a small number of people, you are almost guaranteed to get a 'statistically significant' result." In other words, maybe the five people who ate chocolate already had good cholesterol levels. Maybe they exercised more. Maybe it was just a big coincidence. With a sample that small, it's impossible to know.

That's exactly Bohannon's point. When people were told what they wanted to hear (yay, chocolate!), they didn't investigate further. The study was scientifically dubious, to say the least, but journalists didn't worry about that. Bohannon says the lesson is to be skeptical of anything "studies" claim to prove when it comes to health, especially if the study authors are vague about how many people participated.

The lesson is to always ask questions and find out more before you take life-changing advice from any old blog post.

## Psychic Surgery

It makes sense that people convince themselves chocolate is healthy because they want to believe it. But you can't convince yourself you're cured of cancer, can you? Psychic surgeons say, sure, why not?

Psychic surgery began in spiritualist communities of Brazil and in the Philippines in the 1940s. Spiritualism is the belief that people's spirits continue to exist after their bodies have died. Living people can communicate with the dead, usually through a third party, called a medium. Spiritualism was hugely popular in the United States at the turn of the twentieth century—despite the efforts of skeptics like magician Harry Houdini, who worked hard to expose spiritualists as frauds and con artists. And although spiritualism is no longer the movement it once was, you can still see elements of spiritualism in today's culture. For example, there are TV shows where "mediums" claim to be able to pass along messages from dead relatives.[40]

Psychic surgeons claim to be able to harness the healing power of the spirit world, which enables them to "operate" on patients without actually cutting them open. Although psychic surgery is still mainly associated with Brazil and the Philippines, there are people in the United States and other countries who also claim to be able to perform this service.

For instance, Ray Brown is a construction-worker-turned-psychic-surgeon in England, and he claims that he becomes possessed with the spirit of Saint Paul the Apostle when he does his psychic healing. A UK newspaper article featured a woman who claimed her very serious case of rheumatoid arthritis was completely healed by Brown's spiritual techniques. The article notes that the woman had simultaneously started taking a new arthritis drug, but she told the reporter—apparently with a straight face—that the new medication had nothing to do with her "magical" recovery.

Better yet, some psychic healers claim that the patient doesn't even have to be in the same room. They use the Internet to reach customers and then, after their payments clear, "cure" them psychically without ever actually meeting them.

In traditional psychic surgery from the Philippines—also called "barehand surgery"—the patient does have to be present. While the patient lies on a table, the surgeon reaches inside the body—yes, without gloves—and removes the tumor, tissue, or whatever is causing the illness. Traditional psychic surgery is a fairly gory procedure, resulting in a small pile of mushy, organic matter and lots of blood. But when the blood is wiped away . . . *ta-da*. There is no incision of any kind.

---

[40] If you've ever wondered how these so-called mediums can talk to the dead, you're in luck. "Cold readings" are explained in chapter 4.

Medical organizations decry all forms of psychic healing as utterly fraudulent. Skeptics say it is all a matter of sleight of hand. The surgeon has the tumor and extra blood hidden away (up his sleeve, under the operating table, wherever) and he just makes it appear as

> *"Of all the ghouls who feed on the bodies of the dead and the dying, the cancer quacks are most vicious and most heartless."*
> —*Dr. Morris Fishbein,*
> *editor of the* Journal of the American Medical Association

though it came from the patient. In a blog post defending the practice, one alternative medical practitioner wrote, delightfully, "Psychic surgery is impossible, some say? Yes, but only according to modern scientific standards." All right, then!

The American Cancer Society has been particularly vocal in its critique of psychic surgery. The organization worries that people will trust their cancer care to unproven techniques rather than getting medical care that has some chance of working. For instance the actor Peter Sellers, who played Inspector Clouseau in the old Pink Panther movies, chose to visit psychic healers for his heart condition rather than undergo conventional treatments . . . and died of a heart attack at age fifty-four. A bit later another comedian named Andy Kaufman traveled all the way to the Philippines for psychic surgery on his cancer, which nonetheless is said to have killed him within the year.

That's the real problem with all of these dubious "cures." When patients opt for "miracle" drugs or psychic healing, what treatments are they *not* using that might have a genuine chance of helping them?

## Quacks and Placebos

This chapter has barely begun to scratch the surface of the long list of medical fakes and quacks. Sad to say, I had so much material to choose from in writing this chapter, I had a hard time figuring out where to begin! This raises an interesting—and some would say, pretty troubling—question: Why are we so susceptible to medical quackery?

Given that medicine directly affects how long and how well we live, you might expect people to be extra demanding when it comes to accuracy and honesty. And yet the exact reverse seems to be true! Many people are alarmingly eager to put not only their money "on the table" but their own health as well. What's going on here?

First of all, everybody wants to be healthy. We don't want to get sick, and we certainly don't want to die. Many people turn to medical quacks when they feel traditional medicine has failed them. When doctors shake their heads and say, "I'm sorry, but there's nothing I can do," there is always a quack waiting in the wings, happy to say, "Nonsense! I can save you for the low, low price of $99.99." We believe because we *need* to believe.

## OFF TO SEE THE WIZARD

In June 2014 a US Senate hearing on consumer protection got a visit from a celebrity. Dr. Mehmet Oz, of daytime-talk-show fame, faced intense questioning over his support (some would say "shilling") for unproven diet plans and weight-loss pills. On his show, he has said things like, "I've got the number one miracle in a bottle to burn your fat." He described one supplement as "lightning in a bottle," another as "a magic weight-loss cure."

In November 2012 Oz featured a product he described as "a revolutionary fat buster." As he spoke, the screen behind his head showed the words: "No Exercise. No Diet. No Effort." A more accurate screen might have read: "No Proof. No Science. No Truth."

In his congressional testimony, Oz described himself as a "cheerleader for the audience," speaking "passionately" about products he believed in. However, he also admitted that many of his statements would not hold up under scientific scrutiny.

Dr. Oz's declarations about "miracle" this and "magic" that might have been passionate, but they weren't accurate and they weren't even very original. As we've seen, the good Dr. Oz walked a yellow brick road of medical fakery stretching back to the Middle Ages.

Also, most people are not especially well informed about their bodies. And when you start talking about complex things like, say, the human endocrine system, the average person gets totally lost. This makes it easier for the public to be convinced of something that "sounds reasonable" even if there's no science backing it up.

Quacks also benefit from what's known as the placebo effect. The human mind is very powerful. If someone believes that a cure will work, it often will. People convince themselves they *ought* to feel better, and so they do.

These factors work together to prime people for believing in fakes. Beyond the psychological factors, there's another, physical factor. Many illnesses are what's called self-limiting, which means they clear up on their own. A bad cold might make you miserable, but it's unlikely to kill you. The human body is actually quite good at healing itself, and many illnesses will clear up in time. For this reason it's actually pretty hard for people to truly know whether a treatment worked or not.

Think of it this way: If you buy a toaster, and you put bread in and toast comes out, then you know that your toaster works. But if you have a headache and you take some aspirin, things aren't quite so clear. Did you get better because of the aspirin? Was it the placebo effect? Or did your headache go away for some third reason? You can't really be sure. This opens up a huge opportunity for quacks. People sometimes use particular therapies and then say, "Aha, I feel so much better," when in fact they would have gotten better anyway. As one Dr. Francis J. Shepherd wrote back in 1883, "The medical quack attributes to himself what is due to Nature."

# CHAPTER 8

## Gideon's Trumpet: Deception in War

If deception is an art form, it isn't a particularly noble one. All too frequently the only goal of deceit is to separate people from their money.

But here's a question: What if your goal weren't riches, but something higher? What if the survival of your family, community, or country *depended* on deception? Would that change your view? Or is a faker always a faker?

As you ponder this, consider a few stories from the long history of deception in wartime.

### The Real Housewives of Olympus

The Greek poet Homer gave us a classic story of "deception for a cause" in *The Iliad*, an epic tale about the Trojan War. Later, a Roman poet named Virgil expanded on Homer's story in *The Aeneid*. Our modern understanding of the Trojan War is largely a mix of both men's ideas.

According to the story, a great war was fought between the Trojans and the Greeks.[41] But the whole problem really started up on Mount Olympus, where the ancient gods and goddesses lived and loved and,

---

[41] Or the Trojans and Latins, depending on whether you're reading Homer or Virgil.

more often than not, fought like reality-TV stars. In this case, three goddesses—Hera, Aphrodite, and Athena—argued about who was the prettiest. Their feud spilled over into the human realm and resulted in a siege of the city of Troy that lasted ten years.

After a decade of trying and failing to gain entrance to the gates of Troy, a soldier/carpenter named Epeius executed a deception that would be famous for ages. He built a giant wooden horse—big enough for soldiers to hide inside. The number of men hiding in the horse varies with the telling—some sources say about two dozen; others say fifty or more. In any case the horse was presented at the gates of Troy as a gift. After the Trojans had accepted the gift, the soldiers snuck out of the horse in the dead of night, opened the gate, and the rest was history—as were the Trojans, who all got slaughtered before they knew what was happening.

This story inevitably makes the Trojans look, well, pretty gullible—let's leave it at that.

You might be interested to know that not all of the Trojans were fooled. In Virgil's version, a priest named Laocoön warned his fellow

## FROM THE HORSE'S MOUTH

Experts are not sure how much of Homer's and Virgil's stories were based on real events. The tales were probably inspired by various real-life sieges that took place during the Bronze Age (from 3000 to 600 BCE). Many believe that the real city of Troy was located in what is now Turkey.

And the Trojan Horse? We'll never know for sure. We do know that the ancient Greeks employed a number of very large siege weapons when attacking one another. Because those weapons were made of wood, they were easily set on fire by, for example, a flaming arrow fired by the enemy. To prevent this, the weapons were often covered with animal hides, which were kept wet in order to prevent fires. Could one of these fur-covered siege weapons have been the inspiration for the Trojan Horse?

*A Trojan horse in the town of Canakke, which is near the historical city of Troy.*

Trojans to set the wooden beast on fire. "Do not trust the Horse," he cried. "I fear the Greeks, even when they bring gifts." Before Laocoön could convince his comrades, Athena—who, remember, *started* this whole mess in the first place!—sent two sea serpents to strangle him.[42]

## A Sword for the Lord

Thousands of years ago the Chinese general Sun Tzu wrote *The Art of War*, in which he codified ideas that continue to guide military leaders to this day.

---

[42] The serpents also murdered his two sons, to really drive the point home.

> *"All warfare is based on deception. Hence, when we are able to attack, we must seem unable; when using our forces, we must appear inactive; when we are near, we must make the enemy believe we are far away; when far away, we must make him believe we are near."*
>
> —*Sun Tzu*, The Art of War

Sun Tzu advised warriors to "appear where you are not expected," which sure sounds like what the Greeks accomplished with their Trojan Horse. Sun Tzu also argued that "With the right plan, a small force could beat a larger one." Certainly this concept applies to the biblical warrior named Gideon.

Gideon's story appears in the Book of Judges in both the Christian Bible and the Jewish Torah. Gideon was chosen by God to lead the Israelites against another people called the Midianites. By the way, his name means "destroyer," so you know this is not a guy who messes around.

Gideon and his three hundred soldiers were vastly outnumbered. So Gideon thought up a way to make his tiny army seem massive. He and his men surrounded the enemy camp in the middle of the night. Each soldier held a trumpet and a lamp covered with a clay jar. On Gideon's signal, all the men revealed their lights and blew their trumpets. And they all shouted, "A sword for the Lord and for Gideon!"

The whole racket scared the slumbering Midianites right out of their pajamas. They panicked and, according to the Christian biblical version, ran away *crying*. Gideon and his three hundred pursued the Midianites and killed their leaders.

After his victory, the Israelites begged Gideon to become their king. He refused, arguing that the only true king was God. Very modest behavior for the Destroyer, don't you think? Don't be so sure.

Gideon went on to have many sons, and he gave one of them quite an interesting name: Abimelech. Which means?

"My father is king."

## Welcome to the Working Week

Enough about ancient wars—let's talk about slightly more recent history: Russia, 1380, the Battle of Kulikova. It was then when Commander Dmitry Donskoy essentially pulled a Gideon.

Keep in mind, these were the days when soldiers fought at designated places and at designated times. It was kind of like showing up for work . . . if your job involved being bayonetted.

But not this time. Donskoy tricked his opposition by hiding part of his army in a forest *near* the battlefield. Donskoy approached the field with what appeared to be a pathetically small force. Emboldened, the enemy attacked, and then found themselves surrounded and outgunned when the rest of Donskoy's army came flooding out of the forest.

*Whoops.*

Sun Tzu would have applauded Donskoy for following his dictum: "when able to attack, we must seem unable." However, you don't have to look all the way to Russia for great stories of great deceptions. Depending on where you live, you might not have to look very far at all.

## Damned Yankees

Why do armies resort to deception? Think about the Gideon story. Why go to all that trouble, with trumpets and jars and all that hollering?

Gideon had only three hundred men—that's why. A direct assault would have resulted in total slaughter. Gideon got sneaky because he had to.

The Confederate side of the Civil War was also outgunned by the North much of the time. If they were going to have any chance against those "damned Yankees," they had to get creative.

Take Nathan Bedford Forrest, a Confederate general—and, to his shame, future Ku Klux Klan leader. Forrest had no formal military training but he was good at strategy. In 1864 he needed to take a well-defended Union fort in Alabama with a tiny force. Forrest requested what's called a parley, which is where enemy leaders meet to talk things over but promise not to fight each other. He took Union commander Colonel Wallace Campbell on a tour of the Confederate forces that were gathered outside the fort. After Forrest and Campbell passed by one unit, that unit would quickly pack up its gear and sneak ahead—meaning that Campbell ended up touring the same units again and again, never realizing it was the same men.

With this deception, Forrest managed to convince Campbell that he had four times as many soldiers as he actually had.

So what did Campbell do? He surrendered. That's right—Forrest took the fort with not one shot fired.

## Don't Shoot!

The Quakers, or the Religious Society of Friends, are a Christian sect founded in the 1600s. They are known for being pacifists. They aren't really the sort of folks you expect to have a cannon named after them.

But the Quaker gun, as it's called, is a very special type of gun. It's usually a log painted black and set up to look like a cannon. The point is to convince onlookers that the army has more big guns than it truly does. A Quaker gun is a gun that doesn't fire.

The first recorded use of a Quaker gun was in 1780, during the Revolutionary War, when Colonel William Washington pointed Quaker guns at the redcoats.

During the Civil War, both sides made use of the Quaker gun—the Confederates especially. For instance, in 1862, General Ulysses S. Grant led his Union forces in a siege on the town of Corinth, Mississippi. After a series of battles, the Confederates knew they'd never be able to hold the town. Their leader, General P. G. T. Beauregard, instructed a handful of soldiers to pack up some rations and prepare to attack Grant's forces. He suspected that at least a few of his soldiers would panic, desert the army, and surrender to the Yankees. He was right: the traitors told General Grant all about Beauregard's supposed plans.

Instead Beauregard did something completely unexpected. He transported his men out of Corinth by train. You might think that, in this situation, Beauregard would sneak out of town as quickly as possible. You'd be wrong. When the train arrived to take the soldiers to safety, he told them to make as much noise as they could. They lit fires and played drums. General Grant suspected that, instead of a retreat, a massive collection of *reinforcements* had arrived. Grant became certain that Beauregard was well prepared when he saw all the artillery amassing near Corinth.

If you've been paying attention, you know what those cannons really were: Quaker guns. While Grant hesitated, the Confederates snuck out of Corinth and lived to fight another day.

*Quaker guns—otherwise known as logs—helped guard Centreville, Virginia, in 1862.*

The idea of fake equipment has never gone out of fashion. The battleship HMS *Centurion*, which had been a real fighting ship in the early 1900s, was taken out of retirement during World War II and fitted with fake weapons. Even more recently, fake equipment was used during the Gulf War (1990–1991), when coalition forces wanted to convince Iraqi leader Saddam Hussein that an attack on Kuwait was imminent. Coalition armies used fake equipment and played tank noises over loudspeakers to confuse the Iraqis about where the coalition forces were really headed.

## Follow Their Leader! ... or, Er ... Don't

Sun Tzu said, "Hold out baits to entice the enemy . . . and crush him." In the mid- to late nineteenth century, Native American fighters were masters of this sort of deception. They had to be—their enemy, the US military, had more men and better technology. But the Native American warriors knew their land better than the newcomers, and they were very smart.

You may have heard about Commander George Custer and the Battle of Little Bighorn, where Custer and his men suffered a spectacular defeat at the hands of Crazy Horse and his Lakota fighters. But there was an earlier Native victory—less well remembered today—that leaned heavily on deception.

In 1866 the US Army was attempting to secure the Bozeman Trail. An offshoot of the famous Oregon Trail, the Bozeman Trail took settlers through Wyoming and Montana. It was frequently under attack. The army established three forts along the trail, and Colonel Henry B. Carrington was put in charge.

Serving beneath Carrington was Captain William Fetterman. He and many of his men were skilled Civil War veterans, but they had no experience fighting Native Americans, who were fast and agile on horseback. Where Carrington was cautious, Fetterman was bold—even bragging. "Give me eighty men and I can ride through the whole Sioux nation," he said.

Not everyone agreed with Fetterman's arrogance. A scout named Jim Bridger reportedly told Carrington, "Your men who fought down South are crazy."

The Native fighters and the US Army engaged in small skirmishes for some time. The fighting came to be called Red Cloud's War, after one of the leaders, the Lakota chief Red Cloud. One day in December, ten Lakota and Cheyenne warriors attacked a train bringing lumber to one of the forts. Fetterman and a group of eighty men were sent to defend the train. According to Carrington, they were given strict instructions to *only* defend the train and not engage the Indians.

Instead, when the Indians retreated, pretending to be frightened, Fetterman pursued them. The Indians were led by a young Lakota warrior who would vex the US Army for many years to come. Can you guess who?

## FETTERMAN MASSACRE

Blame for Fetterman's defeat fell on one man: Colonel Henry Carrington, the commander. Carrington spent the rest of his life defending himself.

Remember how Fetterman bragged that he could defeat the entire Sioux nation with only eighty men? That boast was first recorded in a book written by Margaret Irving Carrington, the wife of . . . you guessed it: Henry Carrington. Reports of Fetterman's bad attitude—along with the possibly too-good-to-be-true detail that he died with exactly eighty men—were repeated in books and speeches approved and delivered by Carrington throughout the late nineteenth and early twentieth centuries. Soon Fetterman's reputation as an arrogant fool was well established, relieving Carrington of any responsibility for the massacre.

Fetterman's defenders argue that in choosing to follow Crazy Horse, the captain was just seizing what looked like a good opportunity. They also point to evidence of Fetterman displaying respect for his opponents—not the blind arrogance for which he's remembered.

But with Fetterman dead, Carrington was free to tell whatever story he wanted. This raises the question: Did Carrington add yet another layer of deception to this tale of military trickery?

Crazy Horse, of course. Crazy Horse made sure Fetterman was able to follow him—even slowing down periodically to adjust his bridle, to let Fetterman and his men catch up.

Crazy Horse and his riders were only decoys; they led the soldiers straight into an ambush. There weren't just ten fighters, as it turned out—there were about two thousand, and they were ready. Fetterman's entire squad—the very same number he'd bragged about using to defeat the entire Sioux nation—were slaughtered. The attack took no more than forty minutes. It was the greatest loss the US Army had experienced in the Indian Wars up to that point.[43]

This humiliation ultimately resulted in the 1868 Treaty of Fort Laramie, also called the Sioux Treaty, in which the United States was forced to accede to Lakota demands for greater control over their own land. According to historian Dee Brown, "For the first time in its history, the United States government had negotiated a peace which conceded everything demanded by the enemy and which exacted nothing in return."

## Operation Mincemeat

The ultimate examples of deception come to us from World War II. In fact, you could make a case that the deceptive strategies of the Allied Powers—which included the United States, the United Kingdom, Russia, and others—have never been rivaled.

Many of the Allies' most successful deceptions involved convincing the Nazis that an attack was planned for one spot when in truth the attack was coming from another. In 1943 Britain set out to convince the enemy that an attack on Nazi-occupied Greece was about to occur—when the Allies were actually planning to attack Sicily instead.

Using the codename Mincemeat, British operatives retrieved the body of a man named Glyndwr Michael from a London morgue. Born in Wales

---

[43] Only the Battle of Little Bighorn, in 1876, would be a worse defeat.

in 1909, Michael was homeless and had no family. He died from eating rat poison. (It is not known whether it was suicide or if he was starving and ate contaminated food by accident.)

Michael's corpse was transformed into William Martin, a major in the Royal Marines. He was supplied with identity cards, receipts, personal letters, and a photo of a fake fiancée named Pam. A briefcase was chained to his wrist; inside were supposedly secret details of an imminent Allied attack on Greece.

In April 1943 the body of Martin/Michael was dropped in the sea off the coast of Spain, where he was found by fishermen. A few days after

## EAT YOUR CARROTS

Ever heard that carrots are good for your eyesight? They are high in beta-carotene, which is vital for healthy eyes. But carrots will never *improve* your vision, no matter how many you eat. That fib dates back to World War II.

When the British air force began using radar, the aim of British fighter pilots improved almost overnight. They didn't want the enemy to know why. So rather than let the radar secret get out, the air force created a crunchy orange ruse ("Our fighter pilots sure do love carrots") to confuse the issue.

Or that's one version of the story . . . too bad it's not true, either! The *true* story is more complicated.

During the war many of the foods loved by Brits were not available. But carrots were very easy to grow. So the government tried to convince citizens to eat more of them. Carrots were touted for their nutrition and, notably, for their ability to improve eyesight. Because cities were under constant threat from Nazi bombing, a strict lights-out policy was observed. So the ability to see in the dark was considered a very useful skill. As one official put it, "A carrot a day keeps the blackout at bay."

No matter which way you slice, chop, or shred it, the idea that carrots give you super vision is nonsense. Eat 'em anyway, though—they're delicious!

## AKA ARABEL, AKA GARBO

One of the best double agents was Juan Pujol García. To the Nazis, he was known by the code name Arabel; to the Allies, he was Garbo.

When World War II broke out, Pujol decided he wouldn't stay on the sidelines. He first offered his spying services to the Allies in 1941, but he was turned down—not just once but multiple times. So instead of spying for the Allies, Pujol became a spy for the Nazis, always intending to be a double agent.

The Nazis hired him and sent him to England to report back on the activities of the British military. And so he did, but the information he sent was false—sometimes comically so, like when he claimed the British Navy was practicing maneuvers on a lake that was completely landlocked.

Impressed, the Allies finally hired him. By 1943 he controlled a large network of Nazi spies hailing from all sectors of English society, including a waiter, a student, a businessman, a pilot, a sailor, and an elderly widow. Every one was a fictional character Pujol had invented. Pujol even got the Nazis to pay his "spies." Amazingly, Germany sent regular payments to these imaginary people throughout the war. Pujol turned the funds over to the British treasury.

Martin's "disappearance," the British issued several panicked telegrams inquiring about the location of Martin's briefcase. The news soon reached a Nazi spy named Adolf Claus, who the British believed to be especially gullible.

They were right. In May British agents happily sent this message to Prime Minister Winston Churchill: "Mincemeat swallowed whole." Nazi defenses were reorganized based on the clues they found in the suitcase, which paved the way for the Allies to successfully invade Sicily that July.

## Operation Fortitude

Churchill famously said: "In wartime, truth is so precious that she should always be attended by a bodyguard of lies." As the most precious operation in the war, the Allied invasion of Normandy, France, was attended by a veritable supergroup of bodyguards.

Most important was Operation Fortitude, which was itself divided into separate parts: North and South. The goal of Fortitude North was to convince the enemy that the Allies were planning to attack them in Norway. Meanwhile Fortitude South was designed to protect information about the Normandy plan by convincing the Nazis that the Allies intended to invade Calais instead.

Running so many cons at once presented a number of practical challenges. For one thing, there weren't enough people in Britain to pretend to do all these invasions *and* do the actual invasions as well! This led to the creation of several completely imaginary military forces. One was the First United States Army Group (FUSAG), which was invented in 1943 to create the illusion that a major Allied invasion was planned for Calais. A real general was put in charge of the fake force—the infamous George S. Patton. Initially "Old Blood and Guts" (as Patton was called) was *less* than thrilled about being given command of an imaginary regiment. But since Patton was the most notorious commander in the Allied forces, associating his name with the Calais invasion gave the deception far more weight than it would have had otherwise.

To convince the Nazis that an enormous force was gathering, a massive effort was undertaken to create fake equipment and generate radio traffic suggesting that a lot was going on in the

*Insignia from the various fake divisions that were invented as part of Operation Fortitude.*

Calais area. A film company called Shepperton Studios[44] built a massive storage facility near Dover, across the English Channel from the French town, complete with an oil pipeline to suggest that the British were preparing to make for Calais. The king of England even visited the supposedly state-of-the-art facility—and of course, his trip was excitedly discussed in the media, so the Germans were sure to hear of it.

Meanwhile British diplomats were fed false information to repeat at cocktail parties, so as to be "accidentally" overheard. Large orders were placed for maps of the Calais area, again to leave Nazi spies with the idea that the invasion was planned for that part of France, rather than Normandy.

In the end, Fortitude South was a huge success. So successful, in fact, that the Germans continued to believe that an invasion of Calais was still coming, weeks after the Normandy invasion had occurred! That's why Allied deceptions during World War II are still considered to be some of the best ever attempted. Whether it's a wooden horse in a legend, a dead man on a beach, or a plateful of carrots, the goal remains the same: to keep the enemy confused and off guard.

---

[44] Founded in 1931, Shepperton is probably Britain's most famous movie studio; films made there include *Alien* (1979), *Blade Runner* (1982), *Harry Potter and the Prisoner of Azkaban* (2004), *Star Wars: Episode III* (2005), *Guardians of the Galaxy* (2014), *Avengers: Age of Ultron* (2015), *Beauty and the Beast* (2017), and *Mary Poppins* (2018).

# CHAPTER 9

## Believe Nothing: Mass-Media Hoaxes

Back in 1845, Edgar Allan Poe wrote, "Believe nothing you hear, and only one half that you see." But time and time again, we have proven ourselves unwilling to follow that advice. Ever since there has been a media, there have been media hoaxes.

### The Great Moon Hoax

If you know anything about Edgar Allan Poe, you probably know him as the author of horror stories like "The Tell-Tale Heart" or depressing poems like "The Raven." But Poe was actually quite a hoaxer himself. In 1844 he tried his own balloon-related hoax. Poe penned a newspaper story for the *New York Sun* that claimed a man named Monck Mason had crossed the Atlantic Ocean in just three days by way of a gas-powered balloon. The story was revealed to be a fake just a few days later, and is now included in Poe story collections under the title "The Balloon Hoax." However, Poe's effort paled in comparison to an earlier one: the Great Moon Hoax of 1835.

Before we get into the details of the hoax itself, it's important to understand a few things that were going on in the 1830s. For one thing, it was a period of great advancements in astronomy. Scientists were working on the first map of the surface of Mars; it would be published in 1840. Meanwhile a debate raged in newspapers and scientific journals about whether or not the moon could support life. The Leonid Meteor Showers of 1833 lit up the skies of North America with thousands of meteors—so many, in fact, that some people took it as a sign of the end of the world. In an environment like that, what *wasn't* possible?

Regular people followed these events with great interest—an activity that was made possible by advancements in the printing press. The number of daily newspapers exploded while the cost of the papers plummeted. These "penny papers," as they were called, competed viciously with one another for the reading public's attention.

*An illustration of the Leonid Meteor Shower of 1833.*

And so it was that in August and September 1835, a series of six lengthy articles appeared in the pages of the *New York Sun*. The series was written by Dr. Andrew Grant, and it was titled "Great Astronomical Discoveries Lately Made by Sir John Herschel, L.L.D., F.R.S., etc., at the Cape of Good Hope." The writing was very serious in tone, with an overwhelming amount of scientific detail. The articles were even, most people would say now, a little boring! But the actual content was definitely not.

The series described how a famous astronomer named John Herschel had built a massive telescope in South Africa. The lens of this telescope was about twenty-four feet across, and it weighed more than fourteen thousand pounds. It had an estimated magnifying power of forty-two thousand times the human eye. With this amazing invention, Herschel and his team were able to see the surface of the moon as clearly as though they were looking into a next-door neighbor's window.

According to the articles, the moon had purple mountains shaped like pyramids with bright red caps, and white-sand beaches covered with green stones. Across the landscape wandered herds of blue-gray, goat-like creatures with single horns, as well as beavers that walked around on two feet and built fires inside their dams. There was another creature that had the body of a deer, the head of a sheep, and a bushy, two-foot-long tail.

Most amazing of all were the Moon Men, or Lunarians. They were four-feet tall and covered in short, glossy hair—except on their faces, which were bright yellow. They had wings that stretched from their shoulders down to their calves. Lunarians spent their days lounging around on the moon, eating yellow gourds and red cucumbers. They were, according to Dr. Grant, "very polite."

The articles caused a sensation in New York City. According to the Museum of Hoaxes, about one hundred thousand copies of the story were printed—particularly amazing when you realize that New York only had about three hundred thousand residents at the time! To capitalize on the moon craze, the *Sun* republished the articles as a single pamphlet. It sold about sixty thousand copies in the first month. Other papers began reprinting the *Sun* articles, which created more interest all across the country.

Of course it was all completely fake. There was no such telescope, and there was no Dr. Andrew Grant. Sir John Herschel was reportedly quite startled to hear that he had supposedly seen life on the moon. He hadn't even been anywhere near South Africa in that period![45] It eventually came out that the stories were invented by a British writer named Richard Adams Locke.

We'll never know how many people *actually* fell for the Great Moon Hoax, as opposed to how many simply enjoyed the story for what it was. The mass media was still quite new in 1835, and it seems that most people didn't have the expectations for truth in journalism that we have today. Printing the occasional "tall tale" did not seem as bad back then as it would now.

That said, P. T. Barnum wrote admiringly of the hoax in his 1866 book, *The Humbugs of the World*. And he claimed to have found plenty of people who believed the stories completely. As Edgar Allan Poe later wrote, "The astonishment of the public grew all out of bounds. . . . Not one person in ten discredited it."

In general, readers seem to have taken the hoax in stride. Except for Poe. You see, Poe had published his own version of a "life on the moon" hoax earlier that same year, in a journal called the *Southern Literary Messenger*. But no one fell for it! Poe was certain that his idea had been stolen, and he wrote a lengthy comparison of his own work versus the *Sun*'s, to try and prove his point. He later wrote that he was "astonished at finding [he] could find few listeners—so really eager were all to be deceived."

---

[45] At first, Herschel was amused by the hoax, but in time he became annoyed because people asked about it so often.

Meanwhile, the *Sun*'s chief rival, the *New York Herald*, was definitely not amused. "We mean now to show up the *Sun*," fumed its editorial page, "the impudent *Sun*—the unprincipled *Sun* . . . that cheats the whole city and country." Historians believe the *Herald*'s publisher was mostly upset that he hadn't thought up a moon hoax first.

## The War of the Worlds

It's easy to scoff at the gullible folks of the 1830s. The truth is, we can all be "gotten" if we are approached in the right way.

In the 1930s, the medium of the moment was radio. Many families would gather around their radios every night to listen to music, dramas, comedic skits, and of course, the news. A young actor-director named Orson Welles ran a group called the Mercury Theater on the Air, which performed radio plays, complete with sound effects and live music, for the Columbia Broadcasting System (CBS).[46]

On the night before Halloween in 1938, the Mercury Theater presented an adaptation of the 1898 book *War of the Worlds* by H. G. Wells. The novel tells the story of a Martian invasion of England. The Mercury Theater updated the story, moving the main setting to a tiny town called Grover's Mill, just outside of Trenton, New Jersey. The twist was that the radio play presented the events as though the invasion was really happening.

The show opened with a quick check of the weather, as though this was just another night on the air. The weather report was followed by some fairly terrible music, which an announcer would periodically interrupt with bulletins about explosions on Mars. That was followed by an interview with "Professor Richard Pierson, famous astronomer," played by Welles. The next interruption announced that a meteor had crashed in Grover's Mill. Then aliens emerged from the meteor and began wiping out any humans unfortunate enough to be nearby.

---

[46] Welles's dramatic voice was already known to listeners from his acting on a program called *The Shadow*.

One particularly chilling effect was the simple use of silence. Every once in a while, the broadcast would just cut out completely, leaving "dead air" for a few long seconds before the broadcast would pick up again. At one point, a single lonely voice repeated, "Isn't there anyone on the air? . . . Isn't there anyone on the air? . . . Isn't there anyone?" It was pretty spooky stuff.

The performance had begun with an announcement that said what was to follow was just theater. There was another announcement about two-thirds of the way through the show. And the show concluded with Welles explaining that the show was done for Halloween. Nevertheless, some listeners assumed the broadcast was real. People in the real Grover's Mill ran outside and shot at their own water tower, mistakenly assuming it was a Martian death machine.

The next day the newspapers were filled with the stories of mass panic occurring all over the country. Reports said that the switchboard at CBS couldn't keep up with all the panicked phone calls. In Indianapolis, a woman ran into a church and screamed, "New York has been destroyed! It's the end of the world! Go home and prepare to die!" It was said there were suicides and heart attacks due to the show.

When it became clear that the broadcast was a fake, people were outraged. Much of their ire focused on Welles himself. People assumed he had deliberately tried to terrify his audience. "If I'd planned to wreck my career," he said at the time, "I couldn't have gone about it better."

> "This is Orson Welles, ladies and gentlemen, out of character, to assure you that the War of the Worlds has no further significance than as the [Halloween] holiday offering it was intended to be. . . . We couldn't soap all your windows and steal all your garden gates by tomorrow night, so we did the next best thing. We annihilated the world before your very ears and utterly destroyed CBS. You will be relieved, I hope, to learn that we didn't mean it, and that both institutions are still open for business."
> —Orson Welles, October 30, 1938

A number of the frightening elements were unintentional. For instance, one of the most popular programs at the time was a ventriloquist act by Edgar Bergen and Charlie McCarthy. A lot of people listened to that show from 8:00 to 8:12, and only turned over to the Mercury Theater afterward, meaning that they missed the announcement that the program was fake. Also, because the script for "War of the Worlds" was written in a great hurry, it had a first half that was too long. The result was that the traditional "act break"—like a commercial break on TV—didn't happen at 8:30 as it normally would, but after 8:40. When listeners realized that the broadcast had *skipped* the usual commercial break, well, that was all the proof some people needed.

*The people of Grover's Mill, New Jersey, tend to be pretty good-humored about their town's role in a famous hoax. You can even visit this "Martian Landing Site" monument to the imaginary location.*

In any case, the "War of the Worlds" broadcast remains one of the most famous media hoaxes of all time. But what if I told you there's more to the story? It's actually a hoax within a hoax.

Modern scholars have discovered that there never was any big panic the way newspapers claimed. There's no proof of suicides or heart attacks. Most of the people who called the radio station were complimenting CBS on airing such a good Halloween show. And far from having a ruined career, Welles quickly got a Hollywood contract, producing his classic film *Citizen Kane* just a couple of years later.

So the question is, why did newspapers invent a mass panic that never really occurred? One theory is that newspapers were threatened by the growing popularity of radio. Journalists were all too happy to report that the new medium was dangerous and couldn't be trusted.

## Do Bots Dream of Fake News?

Like any election, the 2016 presidential race involved catchy slogans. Donald Trump's supporters wanted to "Make America Great Again," while fans of Hillary Clinton wore T-shirts declaring, "I'm with Her." But there's another saying that will forever be associated with the campaign: "fake news."

Declaring journalism as "fake news" during this political season became a way to dismiss information listeners didn't like. Don't want to hear that your candidate is behind in the polls? "Fake news!" Don't want to talk about climate change? "Fake news!" But when it comes to social media, fake news is anything but fake.

Social media can connect people who are physically far apart. Unfortunately it can also be used to lie, manipulate, and generally warp our sense of reality. A Twitter or Instagram post might *appear* to have come from a real person, but it ain't necessarily so. Consider "Jenna Abrams," a Twitter account that had about 70,000 followers. "Jenna" spent years tweeting right-wing talking points. But in 2017, it was revealed that "Jenna Abrams" never existed. The account was created and maintained by a company located in St. Petersburg, Russia, pretending to be a young American woman.

"Jenna Abrams" was an elaborate deception. But there are lots of simpler fakes known as bots. A bot is a computer program designed to post automatically. You can often spot a bot by looking at the user profile. You may see a photo that looks like it was stolen from a catalog (because it was), repetitive posts and responses (because bots are dumb), and a user name that looks like a cat walked across the keyboard (what up, @fabbadoodlio232428?).

Also be suspicious of brand-new accounts that suddenly are posting like crazy, and accounts that only post on one topic. Frenzied posting followed by gaps of nothing is another potential sign that the account is being manipulated. And finally, posting at all hours can be a dead give-away—remember, only robots never sleep.

The idea of a mass panic certainly made for a better story as far as Welles was concerned. He bragged of it often. Once he even claimed that the actor John Barrymore was so frightened by the broadcast that he ran outside and released his ten Great Danes, telling them, "The world has fallen, fend for yourselves!"

Researchers aren't sure why the myth of the "War of the Worlds" panic continues to be repeated today. Maybe it's too much fun not to believe!

## Jimmy's World

As noted earlier, readers not named Edgar Allan Poe were pretty good-natured about the Great Moon Hoax of 1835. And despite the urban legend, most of the people who heard the "War of the Worlds" broadcast seem to have appreciated listening to a scary story near Halloween. But standards for accuracy in reporting have changed. These days we expect our news to be factual—at the very least, we expect journalists to *try* to get it right. Unlike in Welles's day, people who invent the news don't end up with Hollywood contracts. *Or do they?*

Let's take the case of Janet Cooke. Growing up in Toledo in the late 1950s, Cooke dreamed of being a writer. She had her own typewriter by age five. And she was ambitious.

Later, when Cooke's journalism career began, she claimed she'd earned a bachelor's degree from Vassar, a prestigious college in New York State. She said her master's degree in journalism was from the University of Toledo. After graduation, she got a job as a reporter for the *Toledo Blade*. Two years later, in 1979, she was hired by the metro section of the *Washington Post*. She informed friends that she fully expected to win a Pulitzer Prize for journalism within three years.

It didn't take nearly that long. On September 28, 1980, the *Post* published Cooke's article, "Jimmy's World," a detailed profile of an eight-year-old heroin addict. Cooke had discovered Jimmy while researching a larger story on heroin, and her editor suggested she focus entirely on the boy. The article talks about Jimmy's life with his mother and her boyfriend, Ron, who is a heroin dealer. Little Jimmy says the experience of using the drug is "like if you was to go on all of [the amusement park rides] in one day." At the end of the piece, Cooke watches as Ron injects heroin into the eight-year-old's arm.

A later article in the *Post* says that Cooke's scandalous article "hit Washington like a grenade." And not just DC—papers all over the country reported on the shocking events described in "Jimmy's World." Everyone asked the same question: Who and where is Jimmy? Even First Lady Nancy Reagan contacted the *Post*, wanting to know if something could be done to help.

Cooke refused to provide any further information about her subject. Her editors at the *Post* backed her up. After all, the interview had been given under the condition of anonymity. As a reporter, Cooke had a responsibility to protect her source.

## THE BALLOON BOY

One October afternoon in 2009, cable news networks brought their usual coverage to a screeching halt. No more talk of wars, politics, or the economy. Instead, they turned their cameras to the sky, following a helium balloon floating over Colorado. For a few hours, that balloon was the biggest news story in the country, possibly the world. Why? Because trapped in the balloon, which sailed about seven thousand miles up into the clouds, was a six-year-old boy.

Or so we thought.

When the balloon landed not far from Denver International Airport, the boy was nowhere to be found. It eventually came out that the child, who came to be known as "The Balloon Boy," was actually hiding in his parents' house the entire time. The whole thing was a hoax engineered by the boy's father. He hoped his son's fame would translate into a spot on a reality show. Instead, the father was sentenced to ninety days in jail and a thirty-six-thousand-dollar fine for lying to police officers.

So the Washington police department opened up a missing persons case on Jimmy. And yet, even with a citywide manhunt under way, the boy could not be found. You can probably guess what was going on.

Some people close to the story were suspicious right away. Courtland Milloy, a fellow *Post* reporter, took Cooke on a tour of the neighborhood where Jimmy supposedly lived. But Cooke couldn't find Jimmy's house. According to Milloy, she didn't even recognize any of the streets. Meanwhile the original editor of the story, Vivian Aplin-Brownlee, also had her doubts. "I knew [Cooke] would be tremendously out of place in a [drug den]," Aplin-Brownlee said later. "No pusher would shoot up a child in her presence."

However, none of these doubts were taken seriously by the upper management of the *Washington Post*. Instead, they submitted "Jimmy's World" for journalism's most prestigious award: the Pulitzer Prize. Cooke was given the prize on April 13, 1981.

It took less than twenty-four hours for the hoax to fall apart. The morning of the prize announcement, a reporter at the *Toledo Blade*, where Cooke had worked years earlier, prepared a short article to celebrate the fact that a former *Blade* writer had won journalism's biggest honor. He noticed that Cook's "official" biography didn't match what the *Blade* had on file about their former coworker. It was soon discovered that Cooke had attended Vassar for only one year. She'd transferred to the University of Toledo to finish her bachelor's, and she'd never gotten a master's degree at all.

With this new information in hand, *Post* editors began viewing earlier concerns about "Jimmy's World" in a new light. Under intense pressure, Cooke finally caved, admitting she'd invented the entire story. In tears, she said, "You get caught at the stupidest things." Apparently she had *heard* of a heroin-addicted boy while researching the story. She was unable to find him, so she invented him instead.

In the end, the Pulitzer Committee took back the prize and gave it to another newspaper. The *Washington Post* apologized and published an extensive investigation into what had gone wrong. Cooke herself resigned from the *Post* and disappeared from the public eye for more than a decade. But she reemerged in the mid-1990s to—you guessed it—sell the rights to her life story to a Hollywood film company for $1.6 million.

## Hoaxes as Art Form: Joey Skaggs

One of our most notorious media hoaxers, Joey Skaggs, began his career as a visual artist in the 1960s. For over forty years, Skaggs has explored the fine line between media hoax and political protest.

Skaggs's initial works were basically just complicated pranks. For example, in the late 1960s tour buses took New York City visitors on guided tours of Greenwich Village so that people could gawk at hippies as if they were animals at a zoo. So Skaggs put together his own tour. He loaded up a busload of hippies and took *them* on a tour of a suburban neighborhood in Queens.

In 1981 Skaggs called a press conference on behalf of a group called Metamorphosis.[47] Calling himself Dr. Josef Gregor, Skaggs said he had discovered a hormone in cockroaches that could be made into a pill that would both cure the common cold and make humans resistant to nuclear radiation. National newspapers ran the headline, "Roach Hormone Hailed as Miracle Drug," and "Dr. Gregor" appeared on TV for interviews.

Over the years, Skaggs has mockingly created a psychic attorney hotline, a business that builds condominiums for fish, and Bad Guys, Inc., a talent agency for actors who specialize in playing villains. Using the name Joey Bones, he created a (fake) vigilante group called the Fat Squad,

---

[47] As far as I can tell, no one at the time noticed the reference to "The Metamorphosis," a story by Franz Kafka about a man named Gregor who turns into a cockroach.

which supposedly intimidated clients into sticking with their diets. In 1992 he convinced reporters that New York City's mayor was hosting a lottery to sell the Brooklyn Bridge. He traveled to London under the name of Baba Wa Simba, where he claimed to be the son of missionaries who had been eaten by lions.

> *"Basically, my work is about this: What do you believe in? How'd you come to your beliefs? Do you ever question the source of your beliefs? If not, why not? . . . I'm a satirist. I'm not just doing a prank, I'm making a satirical commentary, shedding light on things. And there's no death for satire."*
>
> —Joey Skaggs, in a 2016 interview

Skaggs describes himself as a performance artist rather than a con artist, because he doesn't make money off his hoaxes. Many are silly, but some are political. In 2012 Skaggs organized another fake group called Mobile Homeless Homes. Massive, wheeled garbage cans were tied together and pulled through New York City's financial district in an attempt to embarrass big banking firms like Goldman Sachs.

All these hoaxes and more were covered by the national and international media. Reporters interviewed Skaggs over and over again in different disguises, never realizing it was the same person who'd fooled them before.

## Pizza Rat, C'est Moi [48]

When the Ancient Greeks needed a metaphor for the human struggle against insurmountable odds, they had the image of Sisyphus, doomed to push a boulder up a hill for eternity. When New Yorkers wanted a metaphor for the same struggle, they turned to the noble Pizza Rat.

In September 2015 a video was posted to YouTube of a rat dragging a large slice of pizza down a flight of subway stairs. An unseen voice in

---

[48] Pizza Rat is me.

the video encourages the rat's efforts, saying, "Live your best life." The clip quickly went viral, receiving more than seven million views in its first ten days.

Such instant fame always attracts skeptics. But Matt Little, the New Yorker who'd posted the video, denied that the clip was fake. He made a second video mocking the very idea that Pizza Rat could have ever been staged. In that sarcastic clip, called "The Making of Pizza Rat," Little joked that he auditioned many other rats before hiring the one in the video, including Templeton from *Charlotte's Web* and Remy from the Disney film *Ratatouille*.

In January 2016 an article on the site *Gothamist* speculated that Pizza Rat may have been a hoax. The author noticed that Little had an association with a comedy group called the Upright Citizens Brigade. To some observers, this fact alone was sufficient evidence that the whole thing was just a joke.

Either way, the fame of Pizza Rat burned briefly for a short time, only to fade away. Then in late 2016, in the context of widespread concerns over the so-called fake news being shared on Facebook during the presidential election, a new character emerged in the Pizza Rat story. A performance artist known only as Zardulu contacted the *Washington Post* to take credit for the video. She told the reporter that she wanted to distinguish her art projects from political fake news; she argued that those stories were were designed to exploit people, while her hoaxes (she prefers the term "myths") were designed mainly to

charm them. Much like Joey Skaggs, Zardulu told the reporter she wants to make us smile while also reminding us that we shouldn't take what we see at face value.

Zardulu claimed she had created a number of animal-related "myths," such as a staged photo of a raccoon riding an alligator. She also said she'd trained a rat to perform tricks—for example, climbing on sleeping people in subway stations—and that the Pizza Rat video was her creation. However, given that Zardulu only appears in public dressed in a wizard outfit and full mask, it's difficult to know whether to take her claims seriously.

The whole truth behind the video may never be known—and that, to the mysterious myth-builder Zardulu, seems to be part of the fun. But for Pizza Rat's many fans, whether the video is real or fake does not seem to be very important. Admirers of the video say that the trials of Pizza Rat, struggling with a cheesy burden far larger than himself, perfectly capture their feelings about the challenges of big-city living.

## Ain't Necessarily So

Many of the hoaxes in this chapter took place in the context of huge changes in the media, including radical improvements in the printing press, the invention of radio, the expansion of cable news. And, as we see from the Pizza Rat video, mass media is undergoing another revolution, thanks to the internet.

There's a 1993 *New Yorker* cartoon by Peter Steiner that shows a dog sitting and typing at a computer. The caption reads, "On the Internet, nobody knows you're a dog." And it's true: you don't really know for sure who wrote that blog post, or who really owns that Twitter account, or whether that Instagram photo is real or created in Photoshop. This is why catfishing exists. And this is how Internet hoaxes get started.

A favorite type of social-media hoax involves made-up stories about celebrities. Did the singer Justin Bieber really save some Russian guy from

## WHAT'S RUMBLR??.

Apps like Twitter and Facebook are also great spaces for people to invent stories. And instead of long-running hoaxes like the one about beavers on the moon, Internet hoaxes seem to crop up, spread, and quickly die within days or even hours. The list is endless. I barely know where to begin!

- No, blond people are not going extinct.
- No, the Mexican drug dealer known as El Chapo did not threaten to go to war against the terrorist group ISIS.
- No, Hurricane Sandy in 2012 did not result in New York City subways being flooded with sharks.
- No, film director Stanley Kubrick did not confess to helping NASA fake the moon landings.[49]
- There is no app called Rumblr, for people who love fights, nor is there an app called Livr, for people who love alcohol.

The fake stories go on and on. There are entire websites devoted to debunking all this nonsense—the best one in my experience is **www.snopes.com**.

---

[49] For crying out loud, there was no need to fake the moon landings because astronauts actually, you know, *landed there*.

a bear attack? A German tabloid said it happened in 2014 . . . and news traveled all around the world before the story was exposed as a hoax. Did the actors Jeff Goldblum, Natalie Portman, and George Clooney all suddenly die in 2013? Nope, that came from "death hoaxer" Rich Hoover, who spread these rumors through his website. "It started off as a practical joke," Hoover claimed to *E! News*. "But people don't read the fine print, and sure enough, it spreads like mad."

The 2016 presidential election was plagued with lies and hoaxes masquerading as news. Was the US unemployment rate really 42 percent that year? No, try 5 percent. Did Muslim Americans really dance in the streets when the World Trade Center was blown up in 2001? There is not a shred of proof for this. Was Hillary Clinton really at the center of a secret ring of child abusers who communicated with each other through pizza orders? What? Are you even listening to yourself? No. But, alas, social media helped all of these fakes spread like fleas at a dog park.

Another common social media hoax is the classic something-for-nothing post. Is [insert company here] giving away free [great things] to people who repost/retweet/hit "like"/answer a few questions? Maybe, but probably not. This is a popular scam that's used to harvest email addresses and other personal information. This is where we leave the land of hoaxes and venture into the dominion of con artists and fraud.

These days, setting up a professional-looking website is easy and inexpensive. This means criminals can create sites that look legit but are not at all. It's also possible to forge email addresses—people can make it *appear* that they are emailing you from a legitimate company, but they aren't. Just because someone claims to be from a real charity, company, or even government agency, it isn't necessarily so.[50]

In a way, it's a shame that pranksters like Poe and Welles didn't get to experience the Internet. Although perhaps it's just as well—they probably would have been appalled by just how easy it is to trick people these days. So let's wrap things up with a few tips that could keep you from getting fooled in the future.

---

[50] Chapters 2, 4, and 5 offer more information about the Internet and how fakers put it to use.

# CONCLUSION

## News You Can Use

In the minds of most people, the stereotypical victim of fraud is a little old lady who lives alone. She's overly trusting, easily confused, and she totally doesn't understand how the Internet works. This makes her easy prey for con artists. And to an extent, of course, that's true.

But what if I told you that the little-old-lady demographic is not, in fact, the only commonly scammed type of person? It turns out, another commonly scammed type of person looks more like . . . you.

In 2016 the Better Business Bureau reported that young people, especially college students, are actually one of the groups most commonly taken advantage of by scammers. It makes sense, if you think about it: college students are usually living on their own for the first time. As smart as they think they are, they usually don't have much experience making financial decisions.

So let's conclude our investigation of fakers by making sure that, as you grow up and move out on your own, you won't be one of the guys and gals getting gotten.

## That's Not How This Works

Imagine one day you get a phone call from the Internal Revenue Service (IRS). The number on your caller ID looks legitimate. The person on the other end of the call has an important-sounding job title. He informs you that your federal student tax is overdue. And he threatens you with severe punishment—even arrest—if you don't pay up immediately. Sounds scary!

Just one thing: there is no federal student tax.

The real IRS will never, ever just call you up to demand money. Nor will they email you to demand money. They also will not—again, not *ever*—call you to "verify" your tax return or ask you to confirm personal information. The real IRS conducts official business by regular mail. If for some reason you do have a phone conversation with an IRS agent, that would only happen after you've been contacted by mail first. And, again, there's no such thing as a federal student tax.

Scammers also love to call students and make demands about tuition or student loans. This can get sticky, because many students and former students do, in fact, pay a lot of tuition or have overdue loans. And sometimes those loans end up at collection agencies, which have a legal right to try to collect the money. But they do not have a legal right to harass you, and they certainly do not have the right to threaten you with arrest.[51] If you owe money to your school and suddenly start getting phone calls demanding immediate payment, the first thing you should do is contact your financial-aid office. They will help you figure out if the calls are legitimate or not.

Another way scammers steal money from young people is through bogus credit cards and identity theft. Student credit cards are a huge business these days—every college student gets flooded with offers on the first

---

[51] Debtors' prisons were banned under US law in 1833.

day of school, and it doesn't let up from there. Having a credit card is great, but it's important to realize that whenever you apply for a card, you are turning over very important personal information. Experts recommend that students not fill out credit-card applications during public events such as college orientations. It's too easy for someone to get their hands on your personal data and use that information in an identity theft scheme. So if you need that credit card, insist on filling out the application on the credit-card company's secure website. Legit companies will not object to this.

> *Note that the IRS will never:*
> - *Call to demand immediate payment using a specific payment method such as a prepaid debit card, gift card, or wire transfer. Generally, the IRS will first mail you a bill if you owe any taxes.*
> - *Threaten to immediately bring in local police or other law-enforcement groups to have you arrested for not paying.*
> - *Demand that you pay taxes without giving you the opportunity to question or appeal the amount they say you owe.*
> - *Ask for credit or debit card numbers over the phone.*
> —*Internal Revenue Service, www.irs.gov*

Finally, be aware of a phenomenon called friendly fraud. Many college kids live in big dormitories where there are lots of strangers coming and going all the time. They also share rooms with people they may not know very well—and even if you know and trust your roommate, are you sure that you know and trust every single one of your roommate's friends? How about your roommate's friend's cousin or ex-girlfriend? See what I mean? It's really not that hard for a friend of a friend[52] to end up in your dorm room. That's why it's important to keep personal information—and that includes stuff like bills and bank statements—safe from people you don't know.

---

[52] Otherwise known as a stranger!

## If It Sounds Too Good to Be True . . .

Ahh, there's a cliché I bet you're tired of hearing! *If it sounds too good to be true, it is.* Unfortunately history proves that no matter how many times people hear this statement, they never quite believe it applies to them. Humans have been walking into the "too good to be true" buzz saw since the very first caveman/con man sold his friend that "really great cave over the next hill."[53]

College students are no different. Imagine that it's your senior year of high school, and you just got accepted to a wonderful university. You and this school were made for each other. There's just one problem—actually, strike that; there are many thousands of problems, and together they add up to a tuition you can't afford. You start surfing the Internet in search of scholarships. And then it happens: you get an email announcing that *you have already won* a little-known scholarship that you don't even remember applying for. All you have to do is pay a ninety-nine-dollar service charge. What should you do?

This should be an easy one if you've been paying attention! You should delete that email, pronto. The same goes for anyone who pressures you for money *right now*: legit scholarships are not "today only" offers. You should also avoid any scholarship service that promises to locate "secret" scholarships just for you, if you'll pay their membership fee. Information about genuine scholarships is publicly available and easy to search for online.[54]

## Better Smart Than Sorry

I bet you've already heard a lecture or two about "being safe" online. "I know, I know," I hear you cry, "don't give out your address online *blah*

---

[53] There is *still no cave*—didn't we cover this in the introduction?

[54] Of course it is! They want people to apply! Why would you create a scholarship program and then keep it secret? Common sense is your friend here.

## HICKS TRICKS & THROWING BRICKS

Fake scholarships are a serious problem. But even worse is the situation with West Virginia Prep Academy. In that case, it wasn't just the scholarships that were fake, but the entire program!

In 2011 twenty young men, all basketball hopefuls, were found living together in a run-down apartment in Charleston, West Virginia. They had come from all over the United States—as well as from France, the United Kingdom, and Sudan—on the promise of an affordable program with both pro-level basketball training and college courses at nearby Mountain State University. For a five-hundred-dollar application fee, the West Virginia Academy would make all their dreams come true. What the young men got instead was . . . nothing at all. The recruiter, Daniel Hicks, promised a basketball program, but delivered nothing but a two-bedroom apartment with no furniture or even food.

The first attempt to indict Hicks for fraud in 2011 was unsuccessful, but after a federal investigation, Hicks was finally indicted on multiple fraud charges in September 2016. Hicks pled guilty in 2017 and was sentenced to eighteen months in federal prison. Interestingly, the sentence wasn't triggered by the fraud itself. What actually doomed Hicks was when he lied to an FBI agent about the fraud. Big mistake! Of course, while the living conditions in federal prison are far from ideal, they're still better than what he provided for the unfortunate young people who trusted him with their hoop dreams.

*blah blah* . . ." OK, I won't bore you with that lecture again. How about this one instead: don't just be safe online; be smart.

When you go online, you should never forget how easy it is for people to lie to you. Just because . . .

- someone says she's a teenager, that doesn't mean she is. A person with the username CutiePie15 could be a fifty-year-old dude who lives with his mom.
- someone sends you a selfie, that doesn't mean the photo is really of that person. Those perfect pecs and ripped abs may have come straight from a photo archive.

- an email seems to be from a particular account, that doesn't mean it is. Even incompetent hackers know how to fake an email address.
- an article looks like a news report, that doesn't mean it's real. Individuals in the United States and in far-away places like Macedonia have confessed to completely making up "news" stories, for which they get paid every time someone clicks on them.
- a website looks legit, there's no guarantee that it's a real business. Anybody, and I do mean literally *anybody*, can buy a web address and set up a decent-looking site.

Sometimes people lie—or maybe "fib" is a better way to put it—in more subtle ways. Studies have found, for instance, that people tend to make themselves look happier on Facebook than they really feel. Meanwhile people who use dating sites are famous for fibbing about their age and appearance.

All that being said, a 2014 article in *Psychology Today* made the case that most people are actually *more* honest online, because they feel they can express their true selves without being judged. So get out there and make some Internet friends . . . just don't forget to bring your skepticism with you.

## Any Final Words?

I'll be honest: there have been times when researching *Fakers* has been a little depressing. A lot of the stories in this book are funny, but some—from the abusive behavior of Thierry Tilly, to the bald-faced fraud of Daniel Hicks—can make you despair for humanity. Meanwhile, some politicians use the (real and troubling) phenomenon of fictional "news" as a cudgel to attack every legit journalist who writes a story they don't like. But the last thing I want to do is leave you more bummed out than you were when you started reading.

So I hope the takeaway is this: it can be fun to fool others, and as

P. T. Barnum knew, sometimes it's even fun to be fooled. Some fakers, like Orson Welles, just want to entertain us; others, like Joey Skaggs, want to make us think. And then there are those, from Soapy Smith to Bernie Madoff, who only want to make us poorer. Con artists are a creative bunch: I guarantee you that right now, somebody in Dubuque, Iowa, or Lagos, Nigeria, is trying to figure out how to recast the Spanish Prisoner con in a new way. Somebody else is reading the memoir of Charles Ponzi and brainstorming how to devise the latest get-rich-quick scheme that ultimately will enrich no one but the con artist himself.

How do we protect ourselves? Your best weapons are skepticism and common sense. Don't let a hoaxer decide for you what is true or not. Think it through for yourself. Don't immediately believe everything you read online: look for a second source of the same information. Remember that con artists specialize in figuring out what you really want and arguing that only they can provide it—whether it's improved health, unlimited wealth, or a college scholarship. Always remember that in the real world, there is almost never reward without effort. You don't get something for nothing, no matter what advertisements say.

But if you don't believe me by now . . . well, it just so happens there's this totally amazing cave just over the next hill. . . .

# FURTHER READING

Despite my subject matter, I tried to tell you the truth every step of the way. If you want proof, or if you just want to know more, here is a list of sources I used and recommend. The world of fakery, cons, and hoaxes is so vast that there is a ton of material I couldn't fit in. But this is a start!

After a general section, you'll find short bibliographies for each chapter. I didn't include every source I looked at; I'm only mentioning the sources that I recommend to you, my trusted readers. No faking!

## General Resources

Abagnale, Frank W. *Catch Me If You Can*. New York: Broadway Books, 2000.

Barnum, P. T. *The Humbugs of the World*. New York: Carleton, 1866.

Farquhar, Michael. *A Treasury of Deception: Liars, Misleaders, Hoodwinkers, and the Extraordinary True Stories of History's Greatest Hoaxes, Fakes, and Frauds*. New York: Penguin, 2005.

Houdini, Harry. *The Right Way to Do Wrong*. 1906. Reprint, Brooklyn, NY: Melville House, 2012.

Jay, Ricky. *Jay's Journal of Anomalies*. New York: Quantuck Lane Press, 2003.

Konnikova, Maria. *The Confidence Game: Why We Fall for It . . . Every Time*. New York: Viking, 2016.

Maurer, David W. *The Big Con: The Story of the Confidence Man*. 1940. Reprint, New York: Anchor Books, 1999.

The Museum of Hoaxes. www.hoaxes.org

Pascoe, Elaine. *Fooled You! Fakes and Hoaxes Through the Years*. New York: Holt, 2005.

Reading, Amy. *The Mark Inside: A Perfect Swindle, a Cunning Revenge, and a Small History of the Big Con*. New York: Vintage, 2013.

Sifakis, Carl. *Hoaxes and Scams: A Compendium of Deceptions, Ruses, and Swindles*. New York: Facts on File, 1993.

Snopes. www.snopes.com

## Chapter 1
### *Conjurers and Con Artists: Short Cons*

Guttman, Jon. "Soapy Smith: Con Man's Empire." *Wild West*, June 12, 2006.
   http://www.historynet.com/soapy-smith-con-mans-empire.htm

Jay, Ricky. "Tossing the Broads." In *Celebrations of Curious Characters*. San Francisco:
   McSweeney's, 2011.

*The Real Hustle.* "Real Life Scam: The Monte." BBC. September 25, 2014.
   https://www.youtube.com/watch?v=J-aYCYxJDmg

———. "Three Card Monte." BBC. May 2, 2012.
   https://www.youtube.com/watch?v=CwP44S5K4YE

Smith, Jeff. "Alias Soapy Smith: King of the Frontier Con Men." Soapy Smith Preservation
   Trust. http://www.soapysmith.net/index.html

World Bunco Association. "Bunco History." http://www.worldbunco.com/history1.html

## Chapter 2
### *Just Trust Me: Long Cons*

Darby, Mary. "In Ponzi We Trust." *Smithsonian*. December 1998.
   http://www.smithsonianmag.com/people-places/in-ponzi-we-trust-64016168/

Engber, Daniel. "Who Made That Nigerian Scam?" *New York Times Magazine*, January 3, 2014.
   http://www.nytimes.com/2014/01/05/magazine/who-made-that-nigerian-scam.html

Fishman, Steve. "Bernie Madoff, Free at Last." *New York*, June 6, 2010.
   http://nymag.com/news/crimelaw/66468/

Gross, Michael Joseph. "Aristocrats and Demons." *Vanity Fair*, August 2010.
   http://www.vanityfair.com/culture/2010/08/aristocrats-and-demons-201008

Investopedia staff. "What's a Pyramid Scheme?" Investopedia.com. Updated June 14, 2017.
   http://www.investopedia.com/articles/04/042104.asp

Ponzi, Charles. *The Rise of Mr. Ponzi: The Autobiography of a Financial Genius*. Out of print
   but posted online. https://pnzi.com/

Zuckoff, Mitchell. *Ponzi's Scheme: The True Story of a Financial Legend*. New York: Random
   House, 2005.

## Chapter 3
### *Step Right Up! Carnivals and the Prince of Humbug*

Barnum, P. T. *The Life of P. T. Barnum, Written By Himself, Including His Golden Rules for Money-
   Making*. Buffalo, NY: Currier, 1888. https://archive.org/details/lifeofptbarnum00barnuoft

Boese, Alex. "The Cardiff Giant." The Museum of Hoaxes.
   http://hoaxes.org/archive/permalink/the_cardiff_giant

Chicago Historical Society. "Exhibits on the Midway Plaisance, 1893." *Electronic Encyclopedia of Chicago*. http://www.encyclopedia.chicagohistory.org/pages/11421.html

"The Life of Joice Heth, the Nurse of Gen. George Washington (the Father of Our Country)." 1835. *Documenting the American South*. http://docsouth.unc.edu/neh/heth/heth.html

The Lost Museum. http://lostmuseum.cuny.edu/. Online exhibit allowing the user to explore a virtual version of Barnum's American Museum.

Maher, Kathleen. "P.T. Barnum—The Man, the Myth, the Legend." The Barnum Museum. http://www.barnum-museum.org/manmythlegend.htm

Nickell, Joe. *Secrets of the Sideshows*. Lexington: University Press of Kentucky, 2005.

Witter, Bret. *Carnival Undercover*. New York: Plume, 2003.

## Chapter 4

### *Mysterious Minds: Spoon Benders and Psychics*

Biddle, Ken. "Did a Psychic See My Future? No, It Wasn't in the Cards." James Randi Educational Foundation. November 11, 2014. http://web.randi.org/swift/did-a-psychic-see-my-future-no-it-wasnt-in-the-cards

Carroll, Robert Todd. "Uri Geller." *The Skeptic's Dictionary*. http://skepdic.com/geller.html

Cohn, Scott. "Greed Report: They Saw Them Coming: Five Outrageous Psychics." CNBC. July 27, 2016. http://www.cnbc.com/2016/07/27/they-saw-them-coming-five-outrageous-psychic-scams.html

Gresham, William Lindsay. *Monster Midway*. New York: Rinehart, 1953.

Higginbotham, Adam. "The Unbelievable Skepticism of the Amazing Randi." *New York Times Magazine*, November 7, 2014. http://www.nytimes.com/2014/11/09/magazine/the-unbelievable-skepticism-of-the-amazing-randi.html

Menand, Louis. "Crooked Psychics and Cooling the Mark Out." *The New Yorker*. June 18, 2015. http://www.newyorker.com/culture/cultural-comment/crooked-psychics-and-cooling-the-mark-out

Schrager, Alison. "How to Cheat at Everything." *The Economist 1843*, August 16, 2008. https://www.1843magazine.com/story/how-to-cheat-at-everything

WikiHow. "How to Bend Spoons." WikiHow.com, https://www.wikihow.com/Bend-a-Spoon

WikiHow. "How to Cold Read." WikiHow.com. http://www.wikihow.com/Cold-Read

Wilson, Michael. "Seeing Freedom in Their Future, Psychics Reveal All: 'It's a Scam, Sir.'" *New York Times*, August 28, 2015. http://www.nytimes.com/2015/08/29/nyregion/the-secret-to-the-psychic-trade-its-in-the-parole-board-transcripts.html

## Chapter 5

### *Who Are You? Impostors*

Abbott, Karen. "The High Priestess of Fraudulent Finance." Smithsonian.com. June 27, 2012. http://www.smithsonianmag.com/history/the-high-priestess-of-fraudulent-finance-45/

Barnum, P. T. *The Autobiography of P. T. Barnum*. London: Ward and Lock, 1855. https://archive.org/details/autobiographypt01barngoog

Crosbie, John S. *The Incredible Mrs. Chadwick: The Most Notorious Woman of Her Age*. Toronto: McGraw-Hill Ryerson, 1975.

Day, Elizabeth. "I Love You Phillip Morris: A Conman's Story." *Guardian*, September 5, 2009. http://www.theguardian.com/film/2009/sep/06/steven-russell-elizabeth-day-jim-carrey

Dowell, Pat. "Con King Steven Russell: He Still Loves Phillip Morris." *All Things Considered*. NPR. December 3, 2010. http://www.npr.org/2010/12/03/131783406/con-king-steven-russell-he-still-loves-phillip-morris

Seidman, Gwendolyn. "Can You Really Trust the People You Meet Online?" *Psychology Today*, July 23, 2014. https://www.psychologytoday.com/blog/close-encounters/201407/can-you-really-trust-the-people-you-meet-online

Women in History Ohio. "Women in History: Cassie L. Chadwick." *Women in History*. http://www.womeninhistoryohio.com/cassie-l-chadwick.html

Zeman, Ned. "The Boy Who Cried Dead Girlfriend." *Vanity Fair*, April 25, 2013. http://www.vanityfair.com/culture/2013/06/manti-teo-girlfriend-nfl-draft

## Chapter 6

### *I Want to Believe: Science Hoaxes*

Bartlett, Kate. "Piltdown Man: Britain's Greatest Hoax." BBC History. February 17, 2011. http://www.bbc.co.uk/history/ancient/archaeology/piltdown_man_01.shtml

"The Beringer Hoax." *Archaeology*. 2009. http://archive.archaeology.org/online/features/hoaxes/beringer.html

Boese, Alex. "The Lying Stones of Dr. Beringer." Museum of Hoaxes. http://hoaxes.org/archive/permalink/the_lying_stones_of_dr._beringer

D'Costa, Krystal. "The Missing Link That Wasn't." *Scientific American* (blog). April 2, 2004. http://blogs.scientificamerican.com/anthropology-in-practice/the-missing-link-that-wasne28099t/

*Eamonn Investigates: Roswell Alien Autopsy*. 4 parts.
https://www.youtube.com/watch?v=h-LgUFx8xv8
https://www.youtube.com/watch?v=Hi_Tt5luDJw
https://www.youtube.com/watch?v=mW0Fz8wOsGc
https://www.youtube.com/watch?v=AhZvPyGbZ8w

French, Howard W. "Tsukidate Journal; Meet a 'Stone Age' Man So Original, He's a Hoax." *New York Times*, December 7, 2000. http://www.nytimes.com/2000/12/07/world/tsukidate-journal-meet-a-stone-age-man-so-original-he-s-a-hoax.html

Nickell, Joe. "The Story Behind the 'Alien Autopsy' Hoax." Live Science. May 7, 2006. http://www.livescience.com/742-story-alien-autopsy-hoax.html

## Chapter 7
### *Snake Oil: Deception in Medicine*

Armstrong, David, and Elizabeth Metzger Armstrong. *The Great American Medicine Show*. New York: Prentice Hall, 1991.

Bohannon, John. "I Fooled Millions Into Thinking Chocolate Helps Weight Loss. Here's How." *io9*, May 27, 2015. http://io9.gizmodo.com/i-fooled-millions-into-thinking-chocolate-helps-weight-1707251800

Cramp, Arthur J., ed. *Nostrums and Quackery*. Chicago: American Medical Association, 1911. https://archive.org/details/nostrumsquackery00amerrich

Dunbar, Polly. "Psychic Surgeons." *Daily Mail*, August 17, 2014. http://www.dailymail.co.uk/femail/article-2727362/Psychic-surgeons-They-claim-channel-spirits-shrink-cancers-end-chronic-pain-without-picking-scalpel-But-just-preying-desperate.html

Fowler, Gene, ed. *Mystic Healers and Medicine Shows*. Santa Fe, NM: Ancient City Press, 1997.

McNamara, Brooks. *Step Right Up*. Garden City, NY: Doubleday, 1976.

Naro, Maki. "The Red Flags of Quackery." *Science*. 2012. http://sci-ence.org/wp-content/gallery/redflags/redflags_clean.jpg

Pickover, Clifford A. *The Girl Who Gave Birth to Rabbits*. Amherst, NY: Prometheus, 2000.

Serafino, Jay. "Syndrome K: The Fake Disease that Fooled Nazis and Saved Lives." *Mental Floss*, March 29, 2017. http://mentalfloss.com/article/93650/syndrome-k-fake-disease-fooled-nazis-and-saved-lives

Young, James Harvey. *The Medical Messiahs: A Social History of Health Quackery in Twentieth-Century America*. Princeton, NJ: Princeton University Press, 1967. Reprinted online by Quackwatch. http://www.quackwatch.org/13Hx/MM/00.html

## Chapter 8
### *Gideon's Trumpet: Deception in War*

Ambrose, Stephen. *Crazy Horse and Custer: The Parallel Lives of Two American Warriors*. New York: Anchor, 1996.

———. *D-Day, June 6, 1944: The Climactic Battle of World War II*. New York: Simon & Schuster, 1994.

Brown, Dee. *Bury My Heart at Wounded Knee: An Indian History of the American West*. New York: Holt, Rinehart & Winston, 1970.

Gerwehr, Scott, and Russell W. Glenn. "The Art of Darkness: Deception and Urban Operations." Santa Monica, CA: RAND, 2000. http://www.rand.org/pubs/monograph_reports/MR1132.html

Gladwell, Malcolm. "Pandora's Briefcase." *The New Yorker*, May 10, 2001. https://www.newyorker.com/magazine/2010/05/10/pandoras-briefcase

Latimer, Jon. *Deception in War*. New York: Overlook, 2001.

Macintyre, Ben. *Double Cross: The True Story of the D-Day Spies*. New York: Crown, 2012.

——. "Operation Mincemeat." BBC History. bbc.co.uk/history/topics/operation_mincemeat

Monnett, John H. "The Falsehoods of Fetterman's Fight." *Wild West*, October 10, 2010. http://www.historynet.com/the-falsehoods-of-fettermans-fight.htm

## Chapter 9
### *Believe Nothing: Mass Media Hoaxes*

Blanchard, Margaret. *History of Mass Media in the United States: An Encyclopedia*. New York: Routledge, 2013.

Boese, Alex. "The Great Moon Hoax." Museum of Hoaxes. Includes transcriptions of articles. http://hoaxes.org/archive/permalink/the_great_moon_hoax

Boyle, Patrick. "Joey Skaggs Case Studies." The Hoax Project. http://jclass.umd.edu/archive/newshoax/casestudies/professionalhoaxers/Skaggssum.html

Del Signore, John. "Was Pizza Rat a Hoax?" Gothamist, January 7, 2016. http://gothamist.com/2016/01/07/journalism.php

Fitzgerald, Bill, and Kris Shaffer. "Spot a Bot: Identifying Automation and Disinformation on Social Media." *Data for Democracy*, June 5, 2017. https://medium.com/data-for-democracy/spot-a-bot-identifying-automation-and-disinformation-on-social-media-2966ad93a203

History.com staff. "Welles Scares Nation." History.com. 2009. http://www.history.com/this-day-in-history/welles-scares-nation

Ohlheiser, Amy. "She Staged a Viral Story. You Fell for Her Hoax. She Thinks That's Beautiful." *Washington Post*, December 14, 2016. https://www.washingtonpost.com/news/the-intersect/wp/2016/12/14/she-staged-a-viral-story-you-fell-for-her-hoax-she-thinks-thats-beautiful/

Poe, Edgar Allan. "Richard Adams Locke." *Literary America*, 1848. Reprinted by the Edgar Allan Poe Society. http://www.eapoe.org/works/misc/litamlra.htm

Roth-Rose, Spencer. "If You're Reading This, You've Already Been Conned: Joey Skaggs Doc Premieres in LES." *Observer*, June 13, 2016. http://observer.com/2016/06/if-youre-reading-this-youve-already-been-conned-joey-skaggs-doc-premieres-in-les/

Schwartz, A. Brad. "The Infamous 'War of the Worlds' Radio Broadcast Was a Magnificent Fluke." Smithsonian.com, May 6, 2015. http://www.smithsonianmag.com/history/infamous-war-worlds-radio-broadcast-was-magnificent-fluke-180955180/

Skaggs, Joey. "Retrospective." JoeySkaggs.com. http://joeyskaggs.com/html/retsub.html

"War of the Worlds." Recording of original broadcast. https://www.youtube.com/watch?v=Xs0K4ApWl4g

Weisblum, Vida. "Watch Out, New York City: Hoax Master Joey Skaggs Is in Town." *Observer*, June 8, 2016. http://observer.com/2016/06/watch-out-new-york-city-hoax-master-joey-skaggs-is-in-town/

# QUOTATION SOURCES

## Chapter One

Page 7: "Three-card monte . . . game": Ricky Jay, "Tossing the Broads," in *Celebrations of Curious Characters* (San Francisco: McSweeney's, 2011), p. 21.

Page 10: "a great way . . . friends": World Bunco Association, "Bunco History," http://www.worldbunco.com/history1.html

## Chapter Two

Page 20: "$2.50 in cash . . . hopes": Charles Ponzi quoted in Mary Darby, "In Ponzi We Trust," *Smithsonian*, December 1998, http://www.smithsonianmag.com/people-places/in-ponzi-we-trust-64016168/

Pages 21-22: "Ponzi would be a three-day blizzard" [hyphen added]: Neal O'Hara quoted in Charles Ponzi, *The Rise of Mr. Ponzi* (reprint, Naples, FL: Inkwell Publishers, 2001), p. xii.

Page 22: "The scene deployed . . . overnight!": Charles Ponzi quoted in ibid, p. 149.

Page 23: "Well, that's what I did": Bernard "Bernie" Madoff quoted in Steve Fishman, "Bernie Madoff, Free at Last," New York, June 6, 2010, http://nymag.com/news/crimelaw/66468/

Page 28: "brain burglar" and "opened . . . new one": Jean Marchand quoted in Michael Joseph Gross, "Aristocrats and Demons," *Vanity Fair*, August 2010, http://www.vanityfair.com/culture/2010/08/aristocrats-and-demons-201008

## Chapter Three

Page 39: "If it looks . . . about": Bret Witter, *Carnival Undercover* (New York: Plume, 2003), p. 54.

## Chapter Four

Page 45: "There is . . . leaks out": James Randi quoted in *Internet Archive Way Back Machine*, "McGill University Featuring Pseudoscience," http://web.archive.org/web/20110108172522/ http://www.randi.org/jr/200512/123005museum.html#i8

Page 47: "my most influential and important publicist": Uri Geller quoted in Adam Higginbotham, "The Unbelievable Skepticism of the Amazing Randi, " *New York Times Magazine*, November 7, 2014, http://www.nytimes.com/2014/11/09/magazine/the-unbelievable-skepticism-of-the-amazing-randi.html

Page 47: "I am a . . . charlatan": James Randi, in Justin Weinstein and Tyler Measom, *An Honest Liar* (Salt Lake City, UT, and Miami Beach, FL: Left Turn Films and Pure Mutt Productions, 2014), DVD, https://www.amazon.com/Honest-Liar-Justin-Weinstein/dp/B010GLAMNM/ref=sr_1_2?ie=UTF8&qid=1511799240&sr=8-2&keywords=an+honest+liar http://www.worldcat.org/title/honest-liar-truth-and-deception-in-the-life-of-james-the-amazing-randi/oclc/1021083246

Page 48: "If Uri Geller . . . hard way": James Randi quoted in Robert Todd Carroll, "Uri Geller," The Skeptic's Dictionary, http://skepdic.com/geller.html

Page 49: "She was clearly . . . way": Anonymous juror quoted in James C. McKinley Jr., "Psychic Found Guilty of Stealing $138,000 from Clients," *New York Times*, October 11, 2013, http://www.nytimes.com/2013/10/12/nyregion/greenwich-village-psychic-found-guilty-of-stealing-thousands-from-clients.html

Page 50: "just corruption": Sylvia Mitchell quoted in Michael Wilson, "Seeing Freedom in Their Future, Psychics Reveal All: 'It's a Scam, Sir,'" *New York Times*, August 28, 2015, http://www.nytimes.com/2015/08/29/nyregion/the-secret-to-the-psychic-trade-its-in-the-parole-board-transcripts.html

Page 50: "What is . . . baloney?" and "It's a scam, sir": Exchange between parole commissioner and Celia Mitchell quoted in ibid, p. 152.

Page 50: "[It's] a skill . . . want": Tony Ortega in Randall Moldave and Eric Small, "Exorcism," *Penn & Teller: Bullshit!*, season 5, episode 5, directed by Star Price, Showtime video, first aired April 19, 2007, http://www.sho.com/penn-and-teller-bullshit/season/5/episode/5/bullshit-exorcism

Page 51: "one of the . . . me": Debra Saalfield quoted in Jennifer Petlz, "NYC Psychic on Trial on Charges of Conning Clients," ABC Action News, October 4, 2013, http://www.abcactionnews.com/news/state/nyc-psychic-on-trial-on-charges-of-conning-clients

Page 52: "I can spot . . . conned": Simon Lovell quoted in Alison Schrager, "How to Cheat at Everything," *The Economist 1843*, August 16, 2008, https://www.1843magazine.com/story/how-to-cheat-at-everything.

Page 53: "People fall . . . same": William Lindsay Gresham, *Monster Midway* (New York: Rinehart, 1953), p. 119.

Page 55: "Think of . . . crime": Niall Rice quoted in Scott Cohn, "Greed Report: They Saw Them Coming: Five Outrageous Psychic Scams." CNBC, July 27, 2016, http://www.cnbc.com/2016/07/27/they-saw-them-coming-five-outrageous-psychic-scams.html

Page 56: "caused [him] to . . . be": Niall Rice quoted in Louis Menand, "Crooked Psychics and Cooling the Mark Out," *The New Yorker*, June 18, 2015, http://www.newyorker.com/culture/cultural-comment/crooked-psychics-and-cooling-the-mark-out

Page 56: "They're going online . . . mark": Bob Nygaard quoted in Claire Carusillo, "Artisanal Futures," *Racked*, January 12, 2016, http://www.racked.com/2016/1/12/10738276/etsy-psychics

Page 57: "She won't be a psychic anymore": Jeffrey Cylkowski quoted in Tina Susman, "Heartbroken Man Spends More Than $700,000 on Psychics, Chasing After Lover," *Los Angeles Times*, November 18, 2015, http://www.latimes.com/nation/la-na-la-man-fortune-teller-20151118-story.html

## Chapter Five

Page 71: "our kids . . . skeptical": Ephraim Te'o quoted in Ned Zeman, "The Boy Who Cried Dead Girlfriend," *Vanity Fair*, June 2013, http://www.vanityfair.com/culture/2013/06/manti-teo-girlfriend-nfl-draft

Page 71: "the relationship, to me, was real": Manti Te'o quoted in ibid.

## Chapter Six

Page 74: "better versed . . . mind": John Maubray, *The Female Physician* (London: Printed for James Holland, 1724), https://archive.org/details/femalephysicianc00maub

Page 78: "The devil made me do it": Shinichi Fujimura quoted in Howard W. French, "Tsukidate Journal; Meet a 'Stone Age' Man So Original, He's a Hoax," *New York Times*, December 7, 2000, http://www.nytimes.com/2000/12/07/world/tsukidate-journal-meet-a-stone-age-man-so-original-he-s-a-hoax.html

Page 84: "they have monkeys on Mars": Marlon Hines quoted in "The Great Monkey Hoax," The Museum of Hoaxes, http://hoaxes.org/archive/permalink/the_great_monkey_hoax

Page 86: "I almost doubt . . . beak": George Shaw quoted in Penny Olsen, *Upside Down World: Early European Impressions of Australia's Curious Animals* (Canberra, Australia: National Library of Australia, 2010), p. 16.

Page 87: "less than 5 percent": Ray Santilli in "Eamonn Investigates: Roswell Alien Autopsy," YouTube video, 10:02, posted by "UFOHIGHWAY," September 19, 2010, https://www.youtube.com/watch?v=AhZvPyGbZ8w

## Chapter Seven

Page 90: "Quacks abound like Locusts in Egypt": William Smith quoted in Joan Shelley Rubin and Scott E. Casper, eds., *The Oxford Encyclopedia of American Cultural and Intellectual History* (New York: Oxford University Press, 2013), https://brianaltonenmph.com/6-history-of-medicine-and-pharmacy/the-big-picture/quacks-abound-like-locusts-in-egypt/

Page 94: "a veritable 'Who's Who in Quackdom'": Arthur J. Cramp, *Nostrums and Quackery* (Chicago: American Medical Association, 1911), online at https://archive.org/details/nostrumsquackery00amerrich

Page 95: "the dean of twentieth century charlatans": Arthur J. Cramp quoted in James Harvey Young, "Chapter 7: The New Muckrakers," *The Medical Messiahs: A Social History of Health Quackery in Twentieth-Century America* (Princeton, NJ: Princeton University Press, 1966), online at http://www.quackwatch.org/13Hx/MM/07.html

Page 96: "a ten-year-old . . . eight-year-old": Robert Millikan quoted in ibid.

Page 96: "fled like rabbits." Vittorio Sacerdotti quoted in BBC News, December 3, 2004, "Italian Doctor Who Fooled Nazis,"online at http://news.bbc.co.uk/2/hi/europe/4066105.stm

Page 97: "the blind begin . . . walk": Upton Sinclair, "The House of Wonder," *Pearson's Magazine*, September 1922, http://www.worldcat.org/title/house-of-wonder-an-account-of-the-revolutionary-discovery-of-dr-albert-abrams-the-diagnosis-of-disease-from-the-radio-activity-of-the-blood/oclc/170923794

Page 101: "Of all the . . . heartless": Morris Fishbein quoted in James Harvey Young, "Chapter 17: The Most Heartless," *The Medical Messiahs: A Social History of Health Quackery in Twentieth-Century America* (Princeton, NJ: Princeton University Press, 1966), online at http://www.quackwatch.org/13Hx/MM/17.html

Page 101: "Psychic surgery is . . . standards": Patrick Hamouy, "Psychic Surgery and Reiki Healing," EzineArticles.com, June 22, 2007, http://ezinearticles.com/?Psychic-Surgery-and-Reiki-Healing&id=617363

Page 102: "I've got the . . . fat": Mehmet Oz quoted in Jen Christensen and Jacque Wilson, "Congressional Hearing Investigates Dr. Oz 'Miracle' Weight Loss Claims," CNN.com, June 19, 2014, https://www.forbes.com/sites/rosspomeroy/2014/01/10/dr-oz-has-found-16-weight-loss-miracles-so-why-is-there-still-an-obesity-epidemic/#633e24374730

Page 102: "cheerleader for the audience": Ibid.

Page 103: "The medical quack . . . Nature": Francis J. Shepherd quoted in James Harvey Young, "Chapter 20: The Perennial Proneness," *The Medical Messiahs: A Social History of Health Quackery in Twentieth-Century America* (Princeton, NJ: Princeton University Press, 1966), online at http://www.quackwatch.org/13Hx/MM/20.html

## Chapter Eight

Page 107: "Do not trust . . . gifts": *Aeneid* by Virgil quoted in "Beware of Greeks Bearing Gifts," Phrasefinder, http://www.phrases.org.uk/meanings/beware-of-greeks-bearing-gifts.html

Page 108: "All warfare is . . . near": Sun Tzu, *The Art of War*, trans. Michael Evans; Lionel Giles, Laguna Hills: Race Point Publishing, 2017, http://www.worldcat.org/title/art-of-war/oclc/970636118&referer=brief_results

Page 108: "Appear where you are not expected": Ibid.

Page 108: "With the right . . . one": Ibid.

Page 108: "A sword for the Lord and for Gideon!": Judges 7:20 in e Bible (New International Version),] https://www.biblica.com/bible-search/?q=A+sword+for+the+Lord+and+for+Gideon

Page 109: "when able to attack . . . unable": Sun Tzu, *The Art of War*.

Page 112: "Hold out . . . him." Ibid.

Page 112: "Give me eighty . . . nation": William Fetterman quoted in John H. Monnett, "The Falsehoods of Fetterman's Fight," HistoryNet.com, October 10, 2010, http://www.historynet.com/the-falsehoods-of-fettermans-fight.htm

Page 113: "Your men who . . . crazy": Jim Bridger quoted in Mark Felton, *Today Is a Good Day to Fight* (Stroud, Gloustershire, UK: The History Press, 2009).

Page 114: "For the first time . . . return": Dee Brown, *The Fetterman Massacre: Fort Phil Kearny and the Battle of the Hundred Slain.* (Lincoln: University of Nebraska/Bison Books, 1970).

Page 116: "In wartime . . . lies": Winston Churchill quoted in https://www.archives.gov/iwg/research-papers/weitzman-remarks-june-1999.html

## Chapter Nine

Page 121: "Believe nothing . . . see": Edgar Allan Poe, "The System of Dr. Tarr and Prof. Fether," *Graham's Magazine*, November 1845, pp. 193–200, online at http://www.eapoe.org/works/tales/tarrb.htm

Page 124: "the astonishment . . . it": Edgar Allen Poe, "Richard Adams Locke," in "Literary America" (unpublished manuscript, 1848), online at http://www.eapoe.org/works/misc/litamlra.htm

Page 125: "We mean to . . . country": James Gordon Bennett quoted in Alex Boese, "The Great Moon Hoax," The Museum of Hoaxes, http://hoaxes.org/archive/permalink/the_great_moon_hoax

Page 126: "Isn't there . . . anyone?" and "New York has . . . die": Speakers in "Orson Welles–War of the Worlds–Radio Broadcast 1938–Complete Broadcast," YouTube video, 57:02, posted by David Webb, December 16, 2010, https://www.youtube.com/watch?v=Xs0K4ApWl4g

Page 126: "If I'd planned . . . better": Orson Welles quoted in A. Brad Schwartz, "The Infamous 'War of the Worlds' Radio Broadcast Was a Magnificent Fluke," *Smithsonian*, May 6, 2015, http://www.smithsonianmag.com/history/infamous-war-worlds-radio-broadcast-was-magnificent-fluke-180955180/

Page 126: "This is Orson . . . business": Orson Welles in "Orson Welles– War of the Worlds–Radio Broadcast 1938–Complete Broadcast," YouTube video, 57:02, posted by David Webb, December 16, 2010, https://www.youtube.com/watch?v=Xs0K4ApWl4g

Page 130: "like if you . . . day": Little Jimmy quoted in Janet Cooke, "Jimmy's World," *Washington Post*, September 28, 1980, https://www.washingtonpost.com/archive/politics/1980/09/28/jimmys-world/605f237a-7330-4a69-8433-b6da4c519120/?utm_term=.e10e8f86a41b

Page 130: "hit Washington like a grenade": Bill Green, "The Players: It Wasn't a Game," *Washington Post*, April 19, 1981, https://www.washingtonpost.com/archive/politics/1981/04/19/the-players-it-wasnt-a-game/545f7157-5228-47b6-8959-fcfcfa8f08eb/?utm_term=.7d5f0443ea22

Page 131: "I knew [Cooke] . . . in [a drug den]" and "No pusher . . . presence": Vivian Aplin-Brownlee quoted in ibid.

Page 131: "You get caught . . . things": Janet Cooke quoted in ibid.

Page 133: "Basically, my work . . . satire": Jimmy Skaggs quoted in Vida Weisblum, "Watch Out, New York City: Hoax Master Joey Skaggs Is in Town," *Observer*, June 8, 2016, http://observer.com/2016/06/watch-out-new-york-city-hoax-master-joey-skaggs-is-in-town/

Page 136: "It started off as a practical joke": Rich Hoover quoted in Dave Thier, "Eddie Murphy Still Not Dead. Where Do All These Celebrity Death Hoaxes Come From?," *Forbes*, September 4, 2012, https://www.forbes.com/sites/davidthier/2012/09/04/eddie-murphy-still-not-dead-where-do-all-these-celebrity-death-hoaxes-come-from/#295bcaef295b

## Conclusion

Page 141: "Note that the IRS . . . phone": Internal Revenue Service, "Tax Scams and Consumer Alerts," https://www.irs.gov/uac/tax-scams-consumer-alerts

# PHOTO CREDITS

## Chapter One

Page 3: Bosch, Hieronymus. *The Conjurer*. Between 1496 and 1520. Musée Municipal, Saint-Germain-en-Laye. December 7, 2017.
https://commons.wikimedia.org/wiki/File:Hieronymus_Bosch_051.jpg

Page 4: Photo courtesy of the Denver Public Library, Western History Collection; Z-8903.

## Chapter Two

Page 17: cynoclub. Shutterstock. December 7, 2017. Link. https://www.shutterstock.com/image-photo/cute-puppies-purebred-cocker-spaniel-waiting-34291516

Page 24: "Sorry to Leave the Country He Loved." Photo courtesy of the Library of Congress, USZ62-137168.

Page 26: Copyright 1906 by Friede Tower Globe Company.

## Chapter Three

Page 32: "Entering Midway Plaisance to the World's Fair Grounds, Chicago, Ill." Photo courtesy of the Library of Congress.

Page 35: "The wonderful albino family." Photo courtesy of the Library of Congress.

Page 36: "General Tom Thumb." Photo courtesy of the Library of Congress.

Page 41: Bercan, Radu. 378057253. Shutterstock. December 7, 2017. Link. https://www.shutterstock.com/image-photo/vienna-austria-august-09-2015-people-378057253

## Chapter Four

Page 46: Jurvetson, Steve. Photo of James Randi. March 9, 2007. Wikimedia Commons. December 7, 2017. https://commons.wikimedia.org/wiki/File:James_Randi.jpg.

Page 48: McCranie, Jud. Photo of fork bent by James Randi. September 22, 2009. Wikimedia Commons. December 7, 2017. https://commons.wikimedia.org/wiki/File:RandiFork.jpg

## Chapter Five

Page 61: Booth, J. and son. "The Greatest Natural & National Curiosity in the World: Joice Heth."Circa 1835. Somers Historical Society. December 7, 2017. https://commons.wikimedia.org/wiki/File:Joice_heth_poster.jpeg

Page 71: Shotgun Spratling & Neon Tommy. Photo of Notre Dame linebacker Manti Te'o. November 27, 2010. Wikimedia Commons. December 7, 2017. https://commons.wikimedia.org/wiki/File:Mantiteo2010.jpg

## Chapter Six

Page 76: Hogarth, William. "Mary Toft duping several distinguished surgeons, physicians and male-midwives into believing that she is giving birth to a litter of rabbits. Etching by W. Hogarth, 1726." Wellcome Collection. December 7, 2017. https://wellcomecollection.org/works/kqug8gyy

Page 80 (left to right):

"Skull of the 'Eoanthropus Dawsoni' (Piltdown Man)." Wellcome Collection. December 7, 2017. https://wellcomecollection.org/works/zs6y6wgf

"Illustration of Piltdown Man (Eoanthropus). fragments of skull found in 1912." Wellcome Collection. December 7, 2017. https://wellcomecollection.org/works/r24xmve8

"Full face: Restoration of the head of Piltdown Man." Wellcome Collection. December 7, 2017. https://wellcomecollection.org/works/z2afnvxf

Page 82: Haerpfer, Susanne. Photo of the last Tasaday in front of their home. August 24, 2012. Wikimedia Commons. December 7, 2017. https://commons.wikimedia.org/wiki/File:Lobo_und_gruppe_or_wald_322.jpg

Page 85: photoBeard. Shutterstock. 14679058. December 7, 2017. https://www.shutterstock.com/image-photo/model-alien-roswell-nm-1947-14679058

## Chapter Seven

Page 91: Steen, Jan Havickszoon. The Quack. Between 1650 and 1660. Rijksmuseum Amsterdam. December 7, 2017.

## Chapter Eight

Page 107: Nitibhon, Matt. Shutterstock. 116764804. December 7, 2017. https://www.shutterstock.com/image-photo/trojan-horse-troy-turkey-116764804

Page 111: "Centreville, Va. Fort on the heights, with Quaker guns." Photo courtesy of the Library of Congress.

Page 117: U.S. Army Institute of Heraldy. Shoulder sleeve insignia. 1944. Wikimedia Commons. December 7, 2017. https://commons.wikimedia.org/wiki/File:Ghost_Army.jpg

## Chapter Nine

Page 122: duncan1890. "Shower of Shooting stars witnessed in North America." November 04, 2013. iStockphoto. December 7, 2017. https://www.istockphoto.com/vector/shower-of-shooting-stars-gm187096802-29290240

Page 127: ZeWrestler on en.wikipedia. Photo of landing site Grover's Mill, NJ. August 7, 2006. Wikimedia Commons. December 7, 2017. https://commons.wikimedia.org/wiki/File:Landingsite_statue.JPG

# INDEX